A Joyful Path

Books by Thich Nhat Hanh

Being Peace

The Blooming of a Lotus:
Guided Meditation Exercises for Healing and Transformation

Breathe! You Are Alive: Sutra on the Full Awareness of Breathing

Call Me by My True Names: The Collected Poems of Thich Nhat Hanh

The Diamond That Cuts through Illusion:
Commentaries on the Prajñaparamita Diamond Sutra

For a Future to Be Possible: Commentaries on the Five Wonderful Precepts

A Guide to Walking Meditation

The Heart of Understanding:
Commentaries on the Prajñaparamita Heart Sutra

Hermitage Among the Clouds

Interbeing: Fourteen Guidelines for Engaged Buddhism

Love in Action: Writings on Nonviolent Social Change

The Miracle of Mindfulness: A Manual on Meditation

The Moon Bamboo

Old Path White Clouds: Walking in the Footsteps of the Buddha

Our Appointment with Life: Buddha's Teaching on Living in the Present

Peace Is Every Step: The Path of Mindfulness in Everyday Life

Present Moment Wonderful Moment: Mindfulness Verses for Daily Living

The Sun My Heart: From Mindfulness to Insight Contemplation

A Taste of Earth and Other Legends of Vietnam

Thundering Silence: Sutra on Knowing the Better Way to Catch a Snake

Touching Peace: Practicing the Art of Mindful Living

Transformation and Healing:
Sutra on the Four Establishments of Mindfulness

A Joyful Path

Community,
Transformation and Peace

THICH NHAT HANH
and friends

Celebrating the
Twelfth Anniversary of Plum Village,
Thich Nhat Hanh's
Community in France

Parallax Press
Berkeley, California

Parallax Press
P.O. Box 7355
Berkeley, California 94707 USA

Cover photograph by Trân Van Minh
Back cover photograph of Thich Nhat Hanh by Simon Chaput
Calligraphy on back cover and page 61 by Thich Nhat Hanh

Cover and text designed by Ayelet Maida/Legacy Media Inc.
Music scored by David Hauer
Edited by Arnold Kotler

ISBN 0-938077-76-7

Library of Congress Cataloging-in-Publication Data pending

Our deepest thanks to Simon Chaput, Trân Van Minh, and all of the other photographers.
Photo credits: Simon Chaput (pp. 5, 6, 7, 10, 11, 12, 13, 16, 17, 19, 20, 24, 25, 28, 31, 32, 36, 40, 43, 45, 46, 50-51, 54, 58, 67, 68, 79, 82, 83, 87, 93, 99, 103, 105, and 122), Trân Van Minh (pp. 21, 35, 52, 66, 71, 75, 77, 78, 81, 91, 98, 101, 111, and 115), Karen Hagen Liste (pp. 26, 44, 94, and 97), Gaetano Kazuo Maida (pp. 90, 107, 110, 114, and 119), Nancy Rudolph (pp. 29, 33, and 59), Patrick Thornton (page 42), Karen Preuss (p. 72), Therese Fitzgerald (p. 23), courtesy of Sister Chân Không (pp. 47 and 48), courtesy of Ellen Peskin (pp. 57 and 113), courtesy of Plum Village (p. 60)

Permission to reprint the following material is gratefully acknowledged:
"Village of Peace," from *New Age Journal* (April 1992); "Plum Village Summer Opening," from *Yoga Journal* (March 1991), "Spring in Plum Village," *National Catholic Reporter* (July 16, 1993), "Starting Plum Village" and "River Water, Market Rice," adapted from *Learning True Love* (Parallax Press, 1993), "Finding Peace after a Lifetime of War, from *Shambhala Sun* (November 1993), Poems by Thich Nhat Hanh from *Call Me By My True Names* (Parallax Press, 1993), "The Way of the Ancestors," from *The Fruitful Darkness* (HarperSan Francisco, 1993), "Watering the Seed of Mindfulness," from *Ten Directions*, Zen Center of Los Angeles, "Building Sangha," from *Earth's Answer* (Lindisfarne Press, 1975), and a number of other essays from *The Mindfulness Bell* (Community of Mindful Living, Berkeley, California).

Contents

The Good News

Thich Nhat Hanh

The good news
they do not print.
The good news
we do print.
We have a special edition every moment,
and we need you to read it.
The good news is that you are alive,
that the linden tree is still there,
standing firm in the harsh winter.
The good news is that you have wonderful eyes
to touch the blue sky.
The good news is that your child is there before you,
and your arms are available:
hugging is possible.
They only print what is wrong.
Look at each of our special editions.
We always offer the things that are not wrong.
We want you to benefit from them
and help protect them.
The dandelion is there by the sidewalk,
smiling its wondrous smile,
singing the song of eternity.
Listen. You have ears that can hear it.
Bow your head.
Listen to it.
Leave behind the world of sorrow,
of preoccupation,
and get free.
The latest good news
is that you can do it.

Community

"If you are in a good community, one in which people
are happy and living deeply each moment of their day, personal transformation
will take place naturally, without effort.... At Plum Village we do our best
to demonstrate that living peace is something possible."

—Thich Nhat Hanh

Community As a Resource

Thich Nhat Hanh

Living in Harmony

One time the Buddha visited a small community of three monks in a bamboo forest near Kosambi. Anuruddha, Nandiya, and Kimbila were extremely happy to see the Buddha—Nandiya took the Buddha's bowl, Kimbila took his outer robe, and they cleared a place for him to sit next to a yellow bamboo thicket. With their palms joined, the three monks bowed to the Buddha, and the Buddha invited them to sit down. "How is your practice going?" he asked. "Are you content here? Do you encounter difficulties while begging for alms or sharing the teachings?"

Anuruddha answered, "Lord, we are most content here. It is calm and peaceful. We receive ample food offerings, we are able to share the Dharma, and we are making progress in our practice."

The Buddha then asked, "Do you live in harmony?"

Anuruddha replied, "Lord, we do live in harmony, like milk and honey. Living with Nandiya and Kimbila is a great blessing. I treasure their friendship. Before saying or doing anything, I always reflect on whether my words or actions will be helpful for my brothers. If I feel any doubt, I refrain from speaking or acting. Lord, we are three, but we are also one."

The Buddha nodded in assent and looked at the other two monks. Kimbila said, "Anuruddha speaks the truth. We live in harmony and care deeply for each other." Nandiya added, "We share all things—our food, our insight, and our experience."

The Buddha praised them, "Excellent! I am most pleased to hear how you live. A community is truly a community when there is harmony. You demonstrate real awakening."

The Buddha stayed with the monks for a month, and he observed the way they went begging each morning after meditation. Whoever returned first prepared a place for the other two, gathered water for washing, and set out an empty bowl, into which he would place some food in case one of his brothers did not receive enough offerings. After all three monks finished eating, they placed their leftover food on the ground or

Community meeting in the Upper Hamlet of Plum Village

in the stream, careful not to harm any of the creatures who lived there. Then they washed their bowls together. When one of them noticed something that needed tending, he did it at once, and all of them worked together on tasks that required more than one person. And they sat together regularly to share their insights and experiences.

Before leaving the Bamboo Forest, the Buddha told the three monks, "The nature of a community is harmony, and harmony can be realized by following the Six Concords: sharing space, sharing the essentials of daily life, observing the same precepts, using only words that contribute to harmony, sharing insights and understanding, and respecting each other's viewpoints. A community that follows these principles will live happily and in peace. Monks, please continue to practice this way." The monks were overjoyed to spend a month with the Buddha and to receive such encouragement from him.

Taking Refuge Is a Daily Practice

When we were in our mother's womb, we felt secure—protected from heat, cold, and hunger. But the moment we were born and came into contact with the world's suffering, we began to cry. Since then, we have yearned to return to the security of our mother's womb. We long for permanence, but everything is changing. We desire an absolute, but even what we call our "self" is impermanent. We seek a place where we can feel safe and secure, a place we can rely on for a long time.

When we touch the ground, we feel the stability of the earth and feel confident. When we observe the steadiness of the sunshine, the air, and the trees, we know that we can count on the sun to rise each day and the air and the trees to be there tomorrow. When we build a house, we build it on ground that is solid. Before putting our trust in others, we need to choose friends who are stable, on whom we can rely. "Taking refuge" is not based on blind faith or wishful thinking. It is gauged by our real experience.

We all need something good, beautiful, and true to take refuge in. To take refuge in mindfulness, our capacity of being aware of what is going on in the present moment, is safe and not at all abstract. When we drink a glass of water and know we are drinking a glass of water, that is mindfulness. When we sit, walk, stand, or breathe and know that we are sitting, walking, standing, or breathing, we touch the seed of mindfulness in us, and, after a few days, our mindfulness will grow stronger. Mindfulness is the light that shows us the way. It is the living Buddha inside of us. Mindfulness gives rise to insight, awakening, and love. We all have the seed of mindfulness within us and, through the practice of conscious breathing, we can learn to touch it.

Taking refuge in our capacity to wake up is a daily practice. If we wait for difficulties to arise before we begin to practice, it will be too late. When the bad news arrives, we will not know how to cope. If we cultivate our own strengths and abilities by taking refuge in our breathing and our mindfulness every day, several times a day, we will be solid and will know what to do and what not to do to help the situation.

When we cut our skin, our body has the capacity to heal itself. We only need to wash the wound, and our body will do the rest. The same is true of our consciousness. When we feel anger, distress, or despair, if we breathe consciously and recognize the feeling, our consciousness will know what to do to heal these wounds. To practice mindful living is to take refuge in our body, and also in our mind.

The Sangha Is a Jewel
I take refuge in the Buddha, the one who
shows me the way in this life.
I take refuge in the Dharma, the way
of understanding and love.
I take refuge in the Sangha, the community
that lives in harmony and awareness.

Taking refuge in the Three Jewels is a very deep practice. It means, first of all, to take refuge in ourselves. Taking refuge in the Buddha in myself, I vow to realize the Great Way in order to give rise to the highest mind. Taking refuge in the Dharma in myself, I vow to attain understanding and wisdom as immense as the ocean. Taking refuge in the Sangha in myself, I vow to build a community without obstacles.

"I send my heart along with the sound of the bell"

If, for example, you are a single parent and think that you need to be married in order to have stability, please reconsider. You may have more stability right now than with another person. Taking refuge in yourself protects the stability you already have. Taking refuge in what is solid helps you become more solid and develop yourself into a ground of refuge for your child and your friends. Please make yourself into someone we can rely on. We need you—the children need you, the trees and the birds also need you. Please practice going back to yourself, living each moment of your life fully, in mindfulness. Walking, breathing, sitting, eating, and drinking tea in mindfulness are all ways of taking refuge.

Taking refuge in a Sangha means putting your trust in a community of solid members who prac-

---

❋
Discourse on Love

He or she who wants to attain peace should practice being upright, humble, and capable of using loving speech. He or she will know how to live simply and happily, with senses calmed, without being covetous and carried away by the emotions of the majority. Let him or her not do anything that will be disapproved of by the wise ones.

(And this is what he or she contemplates):
  May everyone be happy and safe, and may their hearts be filled with joy.
  May all living beings live in security and peace—beings who are frail or strong, tall or short, big or small, visible or not visible, near or far away, already born or yet to be born. May all of them dwell in perfect tranquility.
  Let no one do harm to anyone. Let no one put the life of anyone in danger. Let no one, out of anger or ill will, wish anyone any harm.

Just as a mother loves and protects her only child at the risk of her own life, we should cultivate Boundless Love to offer to all living beings in the entire cosmos. We should let our boundless love pervade the whole universe, above, below and across. Our love will know no obstacles, our heart will be absolutely free from hatred and enmity. Whether standing or walking, sitting or lying, as long as we are awake, we should maintain this mindfulness of love in our own heart. This is the noblest way of living.
  Free from wrong views, greed and sensual desires, living in beauty and realizing perfect understanding, those who practice boundless love will certainly transcend birth and death.

—Metta Sutta (Suttanipata 1)

---

tice mindfulness together. It is difficult if not impossible to practice mindfulness without a Sangha. Teachers and teachings are important for the practice, but a community of friends is the most essential ingredient. We need a Sangha to support our practice.

When we practice breathing, smiling, and living mindfully with our family, our family becomes our Sangha. If there is a bell at home, the bell is also part of the Sangha, because the bell helps us to practice. Our meditation cushion is a part of our Sangha, too. Many elements help us practice.

We can begin our Sangha-building by inviting one friend to come over for tea meditation, sitting meditation, walking meditation, precept recitation, or Dharma discussion. These are all efforts to establish a Sangha at home. Later, when others wish to join, we can form a small group and meet weekly or monthly. Someday in the future we may even wish to set up a country retreat center. But the practice is not to seclude ourselves for many years in order to attain enlightenment. Real transformation, real enlightenment, is possible only when we stay in touch.

Every Sangha has its problems. It is natural. If you suffer because you do not have confidence in your Sangha and feel on the verge of leaving, I hope you will make the effort to continue. You do not need a perfect Sangha. An imperfect one is good enough. We do our best to transform the Sangha by transforming ourselves into a positive element of the Sangha, accepting the Sangha, and building on it. The principle is to organize the Sangha in a way that is enjoyable for everyone.

Siddhartha, the Buddha-to-be, invited the children of Uruvela village, the water of the Neranjara River, the Bodhi tree, the kusha grass, and many birds and flowers into his Sangha. We have more possibilities available in each moment than we may realize. I know of people in prisons and reeducation camps in Vietnam who practice walking meditation in their cells. We should not miss the opportunity to set up a Sangha. The Sangha is a jewel.

The Art of Sangha-Building
*D*itthadhamma sukhavihari means "dwelling happily in the present moment." We don't rush to the future, because we know that everything is here in the present moment. We know that we have arrived. Walking meditation can help a lot. We walk and touch our deepest happiness. In Plum Village, we always walk mindfully, and we are a bell of mindfulness for others. I practice for you, and you practice for me. Other people are very important.

LA CLOCHE

Tres Lent

Texte et Musique: Jean-Pierre Maradan

We do not have to practice intensively. If we allow ourselves to be in a good Sangha, transformation will come naturally. Just being in a Sang-

Washing clothes by hand

ha where people are happy, living deeply the moments of their days, is enough. Transformation will happen without effort. The most important thing a Dharma teacher can offer his or her students is the art of Sangha-building. Knowing the sutras is not enough. The main concern is building a happy Sangha—taking care of each person, looking into his pain, her difficulties, his aspirations, her fear, his hopes in order to make everyone comfortable and happy. This takes time and energy.

When the Buddha was eighty years old, King Prasenajit, who was also eighty, told him, "My lord, when I look at your Sangha, I feel confidence in the Lord." When the king observed the Buddha's community of monks and nuns and saw the peace and joy emanating from them, he felt great confidence in the Buddha. When we see a Sangha whose practice reveals peace, calm, and happiness, confidence is born in us right away. Through the Sangha, you see the teacher. A teacher without a Sangha is not effective enough. The value of a doctor, a psychotherapist, or a Dharma teacher can be seen in the Sangha around her. Looking at the Sangha, we can see her capacity for helping people.

It is a joy to be in the midst of a Sangha where people are practicing well together. Each person's way of walking, eating, and smiling can be a source of inspiration. If we just put someone who needs to be helped in the midst of such a Sangha, even if that person does not practice, he will be transformed. The only thing he has to do is allow himself to be there. As a teacher, I am always nourished by my Sangha. Any achievement in the Sangha supports me and gives me strength. It is so important to build a Sangha that is happy, where communication is open.

If you don't have a good Sangha yet, please spend your time and energy building one. If you are a psychotherapist, a doctor, a social worker, a peace worker, or an environmentalist, you need a Sangha. Without a Sangha, you will burn out very soon. A psychotherapist can choose among his clients who have overcome their difficulties, who recognize him as a friend or a brother in order to form a group. We need brothers and sisters in the practice in order to continue. In Vietnam we say, "When a tiger leaves his mountain and goes to the lowlands, he will be caught by humans and killed." When a practitioner leaves her Sangha, at some time she will abandon her practice. She will not be able to continue practicing very long without a Sangha. Sangha-building is a crucial element of the practice.

If there is no Sangha in your area, try to identify elements for a future Sangha—your children, your partner, a path in the woods, the blue sky, some beautiful trees—and use your creative talents to develop a Sangha for your own support and practice. We need you to water the seeds of peace, joy, and loving kindness in yourself and others so that all of us will blossom.

Community As Family

Every time I see someone without roots, I see him or her as a hungry ghost. In Buddhist mythology, a hungry ghost is a wandering soul whose throat is too narrow for food or drink to pass through. Hungry ghosts need love, but they do not have the capacity to receive it. They understand in principle that there is beauty in life, but they are not capable of touching it. Something is preventing them from touching the refreshing and healing elements of life. They want to forget life, and they turn to all kinds of intoxicants to help them forget. If we tell them not to, they will not listen. They have heard enough. What they need is something to take refuge in, something that proves to them that life is meaningful. To help a hungry ghost, first of all we have to listen deeply to him or her, to provide an atmosphere of family, and to help him or her experience something beautiful and true to believe in.

Our society produces millions of hungry ghosts, people of all ages. I have seen children just ten years old who have no roots at all, who have never experienced happiness at home and have nothing to believe in or belong to. This is the main sickness of our time. With nothing to believe in, how can a person survive? How can he find the energy to smile or touch the linden tree or the beautiful sky? He is lost, living with no sense of responsibility. Alcohol, drugs, and

In the greenhouse

promiscuity are destroying his body and soul, but he has nowhere to turn. The availability of drugs is a secondary cause of the problem. The primary cause is the lack of meaning in people's lives. Those who abuse drugs or alcohol are unhappy; they do not accept themselves, their families, their society, or their traditions. They have renounced them all.

We cannot be by ourselves alone, we can only "inter-be" with everyone else, including our ancestors and future generations. Our "self" is made only of non-self elements. Our sorrow and

The Five Awarenesses

True love contains mutual respect. In my tradition, husband and wife are expected to respect each other like guests, and when you practice this kind of respect, your love and happiness will continue for a long time. In sexual relationships, respect is one of the most important elements. We are motivated by love and a long-term commitment. But this is only a beginning. We also need the support of friends and other people. That is why we invite friends and family to a wedding ceremony. Everyone joins together to witness the fact that you have come together to live as a couple. The priest and marriage license are just symbols. What is important is that your commitment is witnessed by many friends and both of your families. A long-term commitment is stronger and more long-lasting if made in the context and presence of a Sangha.

Your strong feelings for one another are important, but they are not enough to sustain your happiness. Without other support, what you describe as love may turn into something sour. The support of friends and family coming together weaves a kind of web. The strength of your feelings is only one strand of that web. Every time we have a wedding ceremony at Plum Village, we invite the whole community to celebrate and bring support to the couple. Then, after the ceremony, on every full moon day, the couple recites the Five Awarenesses, remembering that friends everywhere are supporting their relationship:

•We are aware that all generations of our ancestors and all future generations are present in us.

•We are aware of the expectations that our ancestors, our children, and their children have of us.

•We are aware that our joy, peace, freedom, and harmony are the joy, peace, freedom, and harmony of our ancestors, our children, and their children.

•We are aware that understanding is the very foundation of love.

•We are aware that blaming and arguing never help us and only create a wider gap between us, that only understanding, trust, and love can help us change and grow.

—Thich Nhat Hanh

suffering, our joy and peace have their roots in society, nature, and those with whom we live. When we practice mindful living and deep looking, we see the truth of interbeing.

I hope communities of practice will organize themselves in warm, friendly ways, as families. We need to create environments in which people can succeed easily in the practice. If each person is an island, not communicating with others, transformation and healing cannot be obtained. To practice meditation, we must be rooted. Buddhism helps us get rooted again in our society, culture, and family. The Buddha never suggested

Assembling a paper lantern for Full Moon Festival

that we abandon our own roots in order to embrace something else.

Interpersonal relationships are the key to the practice. With the support of even one person, you develop stability, and later you can reach out to others. In Asian Buddhist communities, we address one another as Dharma brother, Dharma sister, Dharma uncle, or Dharma aunt, and we call our teacher Dharma father or Dharma mother. A practice center needs to possess that kind of familial brotherhood and sisterhood for us to be nourished. Aware that we are seeking love, Sangha members will treat us in a way that helps us get rooted. In a spiritual family, we have a second chance to get rooted.

To become a permanent resident of Plum Village, you need the approval of everyone in the Sangha. You have to prove to each brother and sister your willingness and ability to live in peace and harmony. It depends on you and your practice. You need to establish an intimate relation-

ship with at least one Dharma brother or sister for transformation to be likely. We need the kind of love that supports our stability and our transformation. That is why it is so helpful if the community of practice is organized as a family.

In the past, we lived in extended families. Our houses were surrounded by trees and hammocks, and people had time to relax together. The nuclear family is a recent invention. Besides mother and father, there are just one or two children. When the parents have a problem, the atmosphere at home is heavy and there is nowhere to escape, not even enough air to breathe. Even if the child goes into the bathroom to hide, the heaviness pervades the bathroom. The children of today are growing up with many seeds of suffering. Unless we intervene, they will transmit those seeds to their children.

At Plum Village, children are at the center of attention. Each adult is responsible for helping the children feel happy and secure. We know that if the children are happy, the adults will be happy, too. I hope that communities of practice will take this kind of shape in the West, with the warmth and flavor of an extended family. I have seen some practice centers where children are regarded as obstacles to the practice. We have to form communities where children are viewed as the children of everyone. If a child is hitting another child, his parents are not the only ones responsible. Everyone in the community has to work together to find ways to help the children. One adult might try holding the child tightly, not as a policeman, but as an uncle or aunt. Of course, the parents should prevent their child from hitting others, but if they cannot discipline their child, they have to let an uncle or an aunt do it. In the practice center, there should be a garden where the children can play, and there should be people skillful in helping children. If we can do that, everyone—parents and non-parents—will enjoy the practice. If we form practice communities as extended families, the elderly will not have to live apart from the rest of society. Grandparents love to hold children in their arms and tell them fairy tales. If we can do that, everyone will be very happy.

The sun warms Transformation Hall in the Upper Hamlet

Parenting Is a Dharma Door

Nowadays, when things become difficult, couples think of divorce. In traditional cultures, the whole community worked together to help the couple find ways to live in harmony and understanding together. Some people today divorce three, four, or five times. This is an issue that Buddhist practice has to address. How can we create a community that supports couples? How can we support single parents? How can we bring the practice community into the family and the family into the practice community?

If you are a single parent raising your child alone, you have to be both a mother and a father. You have to let go of the idea that you will not be complete unless that "someone" or "something" is with you. You yourself are enough. You can transform yourself into a cozy, stable hermitage, filled with light, air, and order, and you will begin to feel great peace and joy.

A father's love is somewhat different from a mother's. A father says, "If you act like this, you will receive my love. If you don't, you will not get my love." It's a kind of deal. A mother's love is unconditional. As the child of your mother, you are loved by her. There is no other reason. To a mother, her child is an extension of herself, and she uses her body and mind to protect that very soft, vulnerable part of herself. This is beautiful, but it can create problems in the future. Mother has to learn that her son or daughter is a separate person.

It is not easy for a single mother to also be a father, but with a good Sangha helping by being uncles and aunts, you can do your best to play both roles. One day the Abbot of Kim Son Monastery in California said to me, "Thây, you are our mother." Something in me has the manner of being a mother. When I am with children, I can play the role of a mother as well as a father.

Single parenting is widespread in the West. If you succeed in bringing your child up happily, then you can share the fruit of your practice with many people. Single parenting is a Dharma door. Parenting is a Dharma door. We need retreats and seminars to discuss the best ways to raise our children. We do not accept the ancient ways of parenting, but we have not fully developed modern ways of doing so. We need to draw on our practice and our experience to bring new dimensions to family life. Combining the nuclear family with the practice community may be a successful model. We bring our children to the practice center, and all of us benefit. When the children are happy, the adults will be happy also, and everyone will enjoy the practice.

Making Peace with Our Parents

Many people were abused or beaten by their parents, and many more were severely criticized or rejected by them. These people have so many seeds of unhappiness in their consciousness that they do not even want to hear their father's or mother's name. When I meet someone like this, I usually suggest that he or she practice the meditation on the five-year-old child. It is a kind of mindfulness massage.

"Breathing in, I see myself as a five-year-old child. Breathing out, I smile to the five-year-old child in me." During the meditation, you try to see yourself as a five-year-old child. If you look deeply at that child, you see that you are vulnerable and can be easily hurt. A stern look or a shout can cause internal formations in your store consciousness. When your parents fight, your five-year-old receives many seeds of suffering. I have heard young people say, "The most precious gift my parents can give is their own happiness." Because he himself was unhappy, your father made you suffer a lot. Now you visualize yourself as a five-year-old child. Smiling at that child in yourself, you experience real compassion. "I was so young and tender, and I received so much pain."

The next day, I would advise you to practice, "Breathing in, I see my father as a five-year-old child. Breathing out, I smile to that child with compassion." We are not accustomed to thinking of our father as a child. We picture him as having always been an adult—stern and with great authority. We do not take the time to see our father

as a tender, young boy who was easily wounded by others. To help you visualize your father as a young boy, you can peruse the family album and study images of your father when he was young. When you are able to see him as fragile and vulnerable, you may realize that he must have been the victim of someone also, perhaps his father. If he received too many seeds of suffering from his father, it is natural that he will not know how to treat his own son properly. He made you suffer, and the circle of *samsara* continues. Unless you practice mindfulness, you will probably behave exactly the same way towards your children. But if you see your father as himself a victim, compassion will be born in your heart and you will smile. By bringing mindfulness and insight into your pain, your anger toward him will begin to dissolve, and one day, you will be able to say, "Dad, I understand you. You suffered very much during your childhood."

One fourteen-year-old boy who practices at Plum Village told me this story. He said that every time he fell down and hurt himself, his father would shout at him. The boy vowed that when he grew up, he would not act that way. But one time his little sister was playing with other children and she fell off a swing and scraped her knee, and the boy became very angry. His sister's knee was bleeding and he wanted to shout at her, "How can you be so stupid! Why did you do that?" But he caught himself. Because he had been practicing breathing and mindfulness, he was able to recognize his anger and not act on it.

While the adults were taking care of his sister, washing her wound and putting a bandage on it, he walked away slowly and meditated on his anger. Suddenly he saw that he was exactly the same as his father. He told me, "I realized that if I did not do something about the anger in me, I would transmit it to my children." He saw that the seeds of his father's anger must have been transmitted by his grandparents. This was a remarkable insight for a fourteen-year-old boy. Because he had been practicing, he could see clearly like that.

It is important that we realize that we are the continuation of our ancestors through our parents. By making peace with our parents *in us*, we have a chance to make real peace with our real parents.

Returning Home

For those who are alienated from their families, their culture, or their society, it is sometimes difficult to practice. Even if they meditate intensively for many years, it is hard for them to be transformed as long as they remain isolated. We have to establish links with others. Buddhist practice should help us return home and accept the best things in our culture. Reconnecting with our roots, we can learn deep looking and compassionate understanding. Practice is not an individual matter. We practice with our parents, our ancestors, our children, and their children.

There are gems in our own tradition that have come down to us, and we cannot ignore them. Even the food we eat has our ancestors in it. How can we believe that we can cut ourselves off from our culture? We must honor our tradition. It is in us. Meditation shows us the way to do so. Whether we are Christian, Jewish, Muslim, Buddhist, or something else, we have to study the ways of our ancestors and find the best elements of the tradition. We have to allow the ancestors in us to be liberated. The moment we can offer them joy, peace, and freedom, we offer joy, peace, and freedom to ourselves, our children, and their children at the same time. Doing so, we remove all limits and discrimination and create a world in which all traditions are honored.

Some of us do not like to talk or think about our roots, because we have suffered so much. We want something new, but our ancestors in us are urging us to come back and connect with them—their joy and their pain. The moment we accept this, transformation will take place right away, and our pain will begin to dissolve. We realize that we are a continuation of our ancestors and that we are the ancestors of all future generations. It is crucial for us to "return home" and make peace with ourselves and our society.

There is no need to be afraid of going home. It is at home that we touch the most beautiful things. Home is in the present moment, which is the only moment we can touch life. If we do not go back to the present moment, how can we touch the beautiful sunset or the eyes of our dear child? Without going home, how can we touch our heart, our lungs, our liver, or our eyes to give them a chance to be healthy? At home, we can touch the refreshing, beautiful, and healing elements of life.

IN OUT, DEEP SLOW

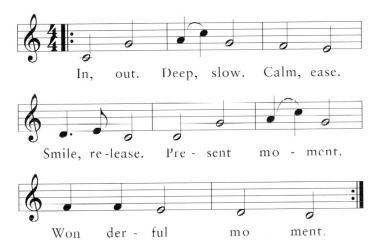

In, out. Deep, slow. Calm, ease.

Smile, re-lease. Pre-sent mo-ment.

Won-der-ful mo-ment.

When we touch the present moment deeply, we also touch the past, and all the damage that was done in the past can be repaired. The way to take care of the future is also to take good care of the present moment.

One Frenchwoman I know left home at the age of seventeen to live in England, because she was so angry at her mother. Thirty years later, after reading a book on Buddhism, she felt the desire to reconcile with her mother, and her mother felt the same. But every time the two of them met, there was a kind of explosion. Their seeds of suffering had been cultivated over many years, and there was a lot of habit energy. The willingness to make peace is not enough. We also need to practice.

Walking meditation

I invited her to come to Plum Village to practice sitting, walking, breathing, eating, and drinking tea in mindfulness, and through that daily practice, she was able to touch the seeds of her anger. After practicing for several weeks, she wrote a letter of reconciliation to her mother. Without her mother present, it was easier to write such a letter. When her mother read it, she tasted the fruit of her daughter's flower watering, and peace was finally possible.

If you love someone, the greatest gift you can give is your presence. The most meaningful declaration we can offer is, "Darling, I am here for you." Without your attention, the person you love may die slowly. When she is suffering, you have to make yourself available right away: "Darling, I know that you are suffering. I am here for you." This is the practice of mindfulness. If you yourself suffer, you have to go to the person you love and tell him, "Darling, I am suffering. Please help." If you cannot say that, something is wrong in your relationship. Pride does not have a place in true love. Pride should not prevent you from going to him and saying that you suffer and need his help. We need each other.

One day in Plum Village, I saw a young woman walking who looked like a hungry ghost. The flowers were blooming everywhere, but she could not touch them. She seemed to be dying of loneliness. She had come to Plum Village to be with others, but when she was there, she was not able to be with anyone. I thought she must come from a broken family, from a society that does not appreciate her, and from a tradition not capable of nourishing her. I have met many people without roots. They want to leave their parents, their society, and their nation behind and find something that is good, beautiful, and true to believe in. People like that come to meditation centers, but without roots, they cannot absorb the teaching. They do not trust easily, so the first thing we have to do is earn their trust.

In Asian countries, we have an ancestors' altar in each home and offer flowers, fruits, and drink to them. We feel that our ancestors are with us. But, at the same time, we are aware that many hungry ghosts have nowhere to go. So once a year we set up a special table and offer them food and drink. Hungry ghosts are hungry for love, understanding, and something to believe in. They have not received love, and no one understands them. It is difficult for them to receive food, water, or love. Our society produces thousands of hungry ghosts every day. We have to look deeply to understand them.

We need two families—blood and spiritual—to be stable and happy. If our parents are happy together, they will transmit the love, trust, and the values of our ancestors to us. When we are on good terms with our parents, we are connected with our blood ancestors through them. But

Sitting after walking meditation

when we are not, we can become rootless, like a hungry ghost.

Transmission has three components—the one who transmits, the object transmitted, and the receiver. Our body and our consciousness have been transmitted to us by our parents, and we are the receiver. When we look deeply, we can see that the three components are one. In Buddhism, we call this the "emptiness of transmission." Our parents did not transmit anything less than them-

he was able to forgive his father. He also realized that if he did not practice mindfulness, the seeds of love and trust in him would remain buried. He made peace with his parents, and through this act, reconnected with all of his blood ancestors.

In our spiritual family, we have ancestors, too, those who represent the tradition. But if they were not happy, if they were not lucky enough to receive the jewels of the tradition, they will not be able to transmit them to us. If we do not respect

Still-Sitting Hut, Thây's hut in the Upper Hamlet

selves—their seeds of suffering, happiness, and talent, which they received, at least in part, from their ancestors. We are very much a continuation of our parents and our ancestors. To be angry at our parents is to be angry at ourselves. To reconcile with our parents is to make peace with ourselves.

An American young man who came to Plum Village told me that he was extremely angry at his father even after his father had passed away. So the young man put a photo of his father on his desk, and practiced looking into the eyes of his father. Doing this, he was able to see his father's suffering and he realized that his father had been incapable of transmitting seeds of love and trust, because he had not touched these seeds in himself. When the young man became aware of that,

our pastor, our rabbi, our priest, we may decide to leave the tradition. Disconnected from our spiritual ancestors, we suffer, and our children suffer, too. We have to look deeply to see what is wrong. When those who represent our tradition do not embody the best values of the tradition, there must be causes, and when we see the causes, insight and acceptance arise. Then we are able to return home, reconnect with our spiritual mentors, and help them.

Through the practice of mindfulness, we can discover the jewels of our spiritual traditions. In Christianity, for example, Holy Communion is an act of mindfulness—eating our bread deeply in order to touch the entire cosmos. In Judaism, mindfulness is there when you set the table or light the Sabbath candles. Everything is done in the presence of God. The equivalents of the Three Jewels can be found in Christianity, Judaism, Islam, and other great traditions. After practicing

❋

The Way of the Ancestors

When I was in Plum Village, after one of Thich Nhat Hanh's Dharma talks in Vietnamese, he invited people to put photos of their deceased relatives in a book placed on the altar. Practicing Buddhism is about discovering ourselves to be in a great flowing river of continuities. Just as our mothers, fathers, and grandparents live inside of us, so do generations upon generations of mothers and fathers before them. Part of our task is to discover how all our ancestors continue to inform our lives, and the same holds true for all forms of life. For we have been shaped not only by our human ancestors but also by the environments in which they lived.

Plum Village, in the old, rich, and fertile Dordogne, feels like very familiar ground to me. I remember coming to this part of southern France as a child in the mid-1950s. I felt right at home then in this place that has been inhabited for tens of thousands of years. Paleolithic peoples used its caves as shrines in which to worship and dream awake the hunt in their depths. Neolithic peoples farmed its rich land. And today, orchards, vineyards, and great fields of sunflowers flow across these old hills. As I sit in meditation each day on a bright ridge overlooking this history, I feel the ancestors of the Dordogne making themselves known to me. I also feel the land itself, the wind and light rain of summer, and the oaks and berries, as well as the brown viper hiding in the thorns. These beings in their generations have been around for a while, too. My senses tell me that I am part of this continuity here in southern France. I have stepped into a river that includes history, and that river also lives inside of me.

—Joan Halifax

❋

There are no stupas, shrines, Celtic ruins, Indian burial grounds here. This is not Lourdes, Chartres, Mont-Saint-Michel, Kyoto, or Bodhgaya. There are no holy temples here, no great cathedrals, no Taj Mahal, Jerusalem Temple, or Mosque. The sacred sites here are in our steps, ourselves, and our stories, slowly enjoyed and soon forgotten. We have nothing to match with our strides but the rhythms of our hearts, and breath, and our loves' limber interbalancing with one another.

—Kate O'Neill

mindfulness, you will be able to return to your spiritual home and discover the jewels of your own tradition. I hope you will do so, for your nourishment and the nourishment of your children. Without roots, we cannot be happy and our children cannot be happy. Returning home and touching the wondrous jewels of our blood and spiritual traditions, we become whole.

Touching the Earth

There is a practice in Buddhism to help us reconnect with our blood and spiritual roots. We bow down and touch the Earth, emptying ourselves and surrendering to the Earth. We touch the Earth with our forehead, our two hands, and our feet, and surrender to our true nature, accepting whatever our true nature offers us. We surrender our pride, hopes, ideas, fears, and notions, and empty ourselves of any resentments we feel. Mind and body work together to form a perfect whole. We prostrate this way six times to help us realize our deep connection to all of our roots.

The First Prostration

In gratitude, I bow to all generations of ancestors in my blood family. I see my father and mother, whose blood, flesh, and vitality are circulating in my own veins and nourishing every cell in me. Through them, I see all four of my grandparents. Their expectations, experiences, and wisdom have been transmitted from so many generations of ancestors. I carry in me the life, blood, experience, wisdom, happiness, and sorrow of all generations. The suffering and all the elements that need to be transformed, I am practicing to transform. I open my heart, flesh, and bones to receive the energy of insight, love, and experience transmitted to me by all my ancestors. I see my roots in my father, mother, grandfather, grandmother, and all ancestors. I know that I am only the continuation of this lineage. I ask my ancestors to support, protect, and transmit to me their loving energy. I know that wherever children and grandchildren are, ancestors are there also. I know that parents always love and support their children and grandchildren, although they are not always able to express it skillfully because of difficulties they encountered. I see that my ancestors tried to build a way of life based on gratitude, joy, confidence, respect, and loving kindness. As a continuation of my ancestors, I bow deeply and allow their energy to flow through me. I ask my ancestors for their support, protection, and strength.

The Second Prostration

In gratitude, I bow to all generations of ancestors in the spiritual family of the Buddha. In myself I see my teacher, the one who shows me the way of love and understanding, the way to breathe, smile, forgive, and live deeply in the present moment. Through my teacher I see all teachers over many generations, all bodhisattvas, and the Buddha Shakyamuni, the one who started this spiritual family 2,500 years ago. I see that the Buddha is one of my teachers and also my spiritual ancestor. I see that the energy of the Buddha and of many generations of teachers have entered me and are creating peace, joy, understanding, and loving kindness in me. I know that the energy of the Buddha has deeply transformed the world. Without the Buddha and these spiritual ancestors, I would have difficulty knowing the way to practice to bring peace and happiness into my life and into the lives of my family and society. I open my heart and my body to receive the energy of understanding, loving kindness, and protection from the Buddha, the Dharma, and the Sangha over many generations. I am the continuation of the Buddha, the Dharma, and the Sangha. I ask these spiritual ancestors to transmit to me their infinite source of energy, peace, stability, understanding, and love. I vow to practice to transform the suffering in myself and the world, and to transmit their energy to future generations of practitioners.

The Third Prostration

In gratitude, I bow to this land and all of the ancestors who made it available. I see that I am whole, protected, and nourished by this land and all of the living beings who have been here, and,

with all their efforts, made life easy and possible for me. I see George Washington, Thomas Jefferson, Abraham Lincoln, Dorothy Day, Martin Luther King, and many others known and unknown. I see those who have made this country a refuge for people of so many origins and colors, by their talent, perseverance, and love, who have worked hard to build schools, hospitals, bridges, and roads, to protect human rights, to develop science and technology, and to fight for freedom and social justice. I see myself touching my Native American ancestors who have lived on this land for such a long time and known the ways to live in peace and harmony with nature, protecting the mountains, forests, animals, vegetation, and minerals of this land. I feel the energy of this land

Annabel Laity, Sister True Virtue, receiving Dharma Lamp Transmission

penetrating my body and soul, supporting and accepting me. I vow to cultivate and maintain this energy and transmit it to future generations. I vow to contribute my part in transforming the violence, hatred, and delusion that still lie deep in the collective consciousness of this society so that future generations will have more safety, joy, and peace. I ask this land for its protection and support.

Sisters Annabel and Jina

The Fourth Prostration

In gratitude and compassion, I bow down and transmit my energy to those I love. All the energy I have received I now want to transmit to my father, my mother, everyone I love, all who have suffered and worried because of me and for my sake. I know I have not been mindful enough in my daily life. I also know that those who love me have had their own difficulties. They have suffered because they were not lucky enough to have an environment that encouraged their full development. I transmit my energy to my mother, father, brothers, sisters, beloved ones, husband, wife, daughter, and son so that their pain will be relieved, so they can smile and feel the joy of being alive. I want them all to be healthy and joyful. I know that when they are happy, I will also be happy. I no longer feel resentment towards any of them. I pray that all ancestors in my blood and spiritual families will focus their energies toward each of them, to protect and support them. I know that I am not separate from them. I am one with those I love.

The Fifth Prostration

In understanding and compassion, I bow down to reconcile with all who have made me suffer. I open my heart and send forth my energy of love and understanding to everyone who has made me suffer, to those who have destroyed much of my life and the lives of those I love. I know now that these people have themselves undergone a lot of suffering and that their hearts are overloaded with pain, anger, and hatred. I know that anyone who suffers that much will make those around them suffer. I know they may have been unlucky, never having the chance to be cared for and loved. Life and society have dealt them so many hardships. They have been wronged and abused. They have not been guided in the path of mindful living. They have accumulated wrong perceptions about life, about me, and about us. They have wronged us and the people I love. I pray to my ancestors in my blood and spiritual families to channel to these persons who have made us suffer, the energy of love and protection, so that their hearts will be able to receive the nectar of love and blossom like a flower. I pray that that person can be transformed so that he can experience the joy of living, so that he will not continue to make himself suffer, and make others suffer. I see his suffering and do not want to see the suffering continue any longer. I do not want to hold any feelings of hatred or anger in myself towards that person. I do not want that person to suffer. I channel my energy of love and understanding to him, and ask all my ancestors to help him.

The Sixth Prostration

In gratitude and compassion, I bow down to my ancient spiritual roots. I see myself as a child, sitting in church or synagogue, ready for the ser-

"This wonderful sound brings me back to my true home"

mon or ceremony—Yom Kippur, Holy Communion. I see my priest, pastor, minister, rabbi, and those in the congregation. I remember how difficult it was to be there and to do things I did not

Peace education

understand or want to do. I know communication was difficult and I did not receive much joy or nourishment from these services. I felt anxious and impatient. Because of the lack of communication and understanding between my spiritual family and me, I left my rabbi, my pastor, my synagogue, my church. I lost contact with my spiritual ancestors and became disconnected from them. Now I know there are jewels in my spiritual tradition, and that the spiritual life of my tradition has contributed greatly to the stability, joy, and peace of my ancestors for many generations. I know those who practice my spiritual tradition were unsuccessful in transmitting it to me, to us. I want to go back to them to rediscover the great spiritual values in my tradition, for my own nourishment and the nourishment of my children and their children. I want to connect again with my ancient spiritual ancestors and get their spiritual energy flowing freely to me again. I see Abraham, Moses, Jesus, Mohammed, and so many others as

my spiritual ancestors. I see teachers over many generations in these traditions as my spiritual ancestors, and I bow down to them all in the present moment.

You Are My Sangha

We need to establish retreat centers where we can go from time to time to renew ourselves. The features of the landscape, the buildings, even the sound of the bell can be designed to remind us to return to awareness. The residential community there does not need to be large. Ten or fifteen people who emanate freshness and peace, the fruits of living in awareness, are enough. When we are there, they care for us, console us, support us, and help us heal our wounds. Even when we cannot actually go there, just thinking of the center makes us smile and feel more at peace.

BREATHING IN, BREATHING OUT

Breath-ing in, breath-ing out. Breath-ing
in, breath-ing out. I am bloom-ing as a
flow-er. I am fresh as the dew. I am
sol-id as a moun-tain. I am firm as the
earth. I am free. Breath-ing
in, breath-ing out. Breath-ing in, breath-ing
out. I am wa-ter re-flect-ing what is
real, what is true, and I feel there is
space deep in-side of me. I am
free, I am free, I am free.

The residents can organize larger retreats occasionally to teach the art of enjoying life and taking care of each other. Mindful living is an art, and a retreat center can be a place where joy and happiness are authentic. The community can also offer Days of Mindfulness for people to come and live happily together for one day, and they can organize study courses on mindfulness, conscious breathing, Buddhist psychology, and transformation. We must work together with everyone in peace and harmony. Using each person's talents and ideas, we can organize retreats and Days of Mindfulness that children and adults love and want to practice more.

Most of the retreats can be for preventive practice, developing the habit of practicing mindfulness before things get too bad. But some retreats should be for those who are undergoing extreme suffering, although even then two-thirds of the retreatants should be healthy and stable for the practice to succeed. The depth and substance of the practice are the most important. The forms can be adapted.

At the retreat center, we can enjoy doing everything in mindfulness, and our friends will see the value of the practice through us—not through what we say, but through our being. We can also enjoy the practice at home, at work, or at school. For the practice to succeed, we have to find ways to incorporate it into our daily lives. Going to a retreat center from time to time can help a lot. Forming a Sangha at home is crucial.

Two thousand, five hundred years ago, the Buddha Shakyamuni predicted that the next Buddha will be named Maitreya, the "Buddha of Love." I think the Buddha of Love may be born as a community and not just as an individual. Communities of mindful living are crucial for our survival and the survival of our planet. A good Sangha can help us resist the speed, violence, and unwholesome ways of our time. Mindfulness protects us and keeps us going in the direction of harmony and awareness. We need the support of friends in the practice. You are my Sangha. Let us take good care of each other.

Village of Peace

Linda Ilene Solomon

A slight, poised man in a gray overcoat, woolen cap, and clogs walks slowly, very slowly, up a muddy roadside path in the French countryside, stopping to pick up an autumn leaf. It is drizzling. A group of about forty of us are following the man, walking when he walks, stopping when he stops. We wait to watch the man's gentle, precise movements, the way he turns the leaf over in his hand, as if the brittle edges and brilliant shadings contain in their subtleties the mysteries of the world. The man smiles, looks up for a moment. The sky is wet with fog. He holds the leaf against his heart and stands still, as if he has an eternity to get down the path.

The man on the path is Thich Nhat Hanh, one of the most beloved Buddhist teachers in the West. And the walk is no ordinary walk. It is a walking meditation, a step toward what this Vietnamese Zen monk calls "real strength," a walk toward "being peace" led by one of the most intriguing peace activists of our time. The setting for this walk is Plum Village, the Buddhist community and retreat center that Nhat Hanh founded twelve years ago among the vineyards and farmlands near Bordeaux. It has become a mecca of sorts for peace workers, wartime refugees, even battlefield veterans. Others visit seeking to learn ways to integrate their spirituality into social action.

Sixty-seven-year-old Nhat Hanh—known as Thây ("teacher," pronounced like "tie") by his students—is a rare combination of mystic, scholar, and activist. From his years as a young monk working in the maelstrom of the Vietnam War to his current calling as a philosopher, poet, author, and teacher, he has preached a form of Buddhism—a unique blend of religion and social action that he calls "engaged Buddhism"—that has compelling relevance for the world today. This is a man who believes in "bodhisattva action" that enlightenment can come to no one as long as one being continues to suffer. Strengthened by a

Entry to the Lower Hamlet

belief that greed, hatred, and violence are the enemies—never people—Nhat Hanh has repeatedly risked his life to help people who are suffering.

Walking meditation, which joins awareness with conscious breathing, is one of Nhat Hanh's most essential practices. He calls this practice

Sister Chân Không

"mindfulness" and believes that it can help heal people in every aspect of life. "The future of human beings depends on your steps," Nhat Hanh once wrote. "We [as a race] are like sleep-walkers, not knowing what we are doing or where we are heading. Whether human beings can wake up or not depends on whether we can take conscientious and mindful steps. That is why the future of human beings, as well as the future of all life on this Earth, depends on your steps. Let's transform every path on this Earth to a path for walking meditation."

Waiting for Nhat Hanh to take his next step, I survey the silent procession on the road. Nhat Hanh, still holding the leaf against his heart, is gazing out on the orchard, as if discovering for the very first time the beauty of the fields. Standing beside Nhat Hanh is his assistant, Sister Chân Không, statuesque in her old, dark coat and scuffed clogs, her large, dark eyes cast downward. The rest of our group includes Vietnamese

monks, nuns, and refugees along with Western social workers, peace activists, and students. Year by year, this peacemaking center draws more and more Americans and Europeans for visits.

Nhat Hanh smiles again and raises his eyes. I breathe deeply, following his gaze to the sky. After a moment he proceeds along the road and the rest of us follow, breathing in and out purposefully with each step, relaxing so deeply that the world seems to slow down.

Plum Village evolved from an idea that Nhat Hanh had while working as a peace activist during the war in Vietnam. At that time he was the organizer of the Peace Corps-like School of Youth for Social Service (SYSS), which served as Vietnam's main training program for Buddhist peace workers. Inspired by the Gandhian movement in India, the SYSS espoused a philosophy of decentralization for solving problems of agriculture, health care, sanitation, and education. The program's hundreds of volunteers helped build schools and health clinics—and rebuild villages destroyed by American bombs.

During those war-torn times, Nhat Hanh envisioned creating a community where peace workers could meet, share ideas, heal, and go back out into the world rejuvenated to continue their work. His plan was thwarted, however, after he went to the United States to plead for peace. When the monk's stay in America was to draw to a close, the government of South Vietnam forbade him to return home. Nhat Hanh and his colleagues at the Unified Buddhist Church of Vietnam were considered enemies by both the Communists and the American-backed Diêm regime. Their ability to win the hearts of the Vietnamese, nearly all of whom were Buddhist, and to rally thousands of people to nonviolent action threatened the military on both sides.

While Nhat Hanh was being seen as a political threat in his homeland, his message was earning him friends in the United States. His visit with Martin Luther King, Jr., convinced the civil rights leader to publicly condemn the war. (Later, King would nominate Nhat Hanh for the Nobel Peace Prize, saying, "I do not personally know of anyone more worthy of the Nobel Peace Prize than this gentle Buddhist monk from Vietnam.") Nhat

Hanh also kindled a friendship with the Catholic mystic and writer Thomas Merton, who later composed an essay, "Nhat Hanh Is My Brother," in which he observed that the monk "has shown us that Zen is not an esoteric and world denying cult of inner illumination, but that it has its rare and unique sense of responsibility in the modern world."

Nhat Hanh's appeal was not limited to religious leaders and peacemakers. During his trip to the United States, he went to Washington to voice his country's despair to Secretary of Defense Robert McNamara. "You can win only by destroying all of us," Nhat Hanh told McNamara, who found the soft-spoken monk so appealing that he canceled his next appointment so he could continue to sit and talk with him.

"I said, 'Liberate us from your liberation,'" Nhat Hanh recalls.

When the war ended, Nhat Hanh remained in exile, first in Paris, then for several years on a small farm a hundred miles from Paris before founding Plum Village: two farms, an upper hamlet and lower hamlet about a mile apart, a collection of old stone farm buildings and 1,250 plum trees—a total of eighty acres. In its twelve years Plum Village has grown into what Nhat Hanh calls "a practice center," a place that "offers people the occasion to look at their life more deeply, at their real problems."

En route to Plum Village

Evening meditation, Transformation Hall

Though Plum Village is year-round home to just thirty Vietnamese monks, nuns, laypeople, and a dozen Westerners—and their daily Zen practice—the wide appeal of Nhat Hanh and his teaching brings many visitors and short-term residents through the community. The Lower Hamlet often is inhabited by Vietnamese families new to the West who are struggling to bridge gaps both cultural and generational: the younger family members know no home other than North America or Europe, whereas the elders are feeling the loss of their homeland. During the summer, when Plum Village opens its doors on July 15 for a month-long celebration, a thousand people come and go; indoor accommodations fill up, and tents speckle the fields around the village.

Peace activists come to Plum Village for instruction and encouragement in nonpartisan peacemaking. American veterans of the Vietnam War come to learn to live in the present. Vietnamese in exile come to heal wounds suffered during the war during forced "reeducation" by the communists, during harrowing escapes by boat through unfriendly seas. For all who visit, it is a place to learn how to nourish oneself with peace every day.

"We try to demonstrate that living peace is something possible," says Nhat Hanh. "Practicing harmony and understanding is something you can do in a family or in a group of friends. When you are able to demonstrate that, people will have faith. They can see something wholesome to cling on, to believe in, and they will do the same thing elsewhere. This is hope. We need hope and confidence."

At Plum Village, monks, nuns, and visitors alike follow a regimen that is both ancient and modern. Though Nhat Hanh has ties to a spiritual lineage that goes back generations, he has be-

The community gathers to discuss the day's work needs

come known for teaching students to read Buddhist scriptures with a modern eye and for imbuing old rituals with new meaning for everyday life. When Christians and Jews from the West come to the community, he encourages them to "water the good seeds" of their roots, to take what they learn from him and from Buddhism and apply it to their own cultures. "Many young people who come from the West seem to find it necessary to reject their own culture," says Nhat Hanh. "They tend to be alienated by their own culture. We want them to go back to their culture to get integrated again. Maybe the practice of mindfulness can help them rediscover the best things in Western culture."

In this community the practice of mindfulness is not just a part of morning meditation sessions or afternoon Dharma talks. It is an all-day prac-

tice. Every fifteen minutes the mindfulness bells ring, signaling a time to stop all talking for a moment, to breathe in and out consciously a few times, and to relax. Even when the telephone rings, everyone stops what they're doing and remains still until the phone rings four times. "The bell makes life worth living for us," says Sister Annabel Laity, a British nun who is one of the community's three ordained teachers (along with Sisters Chân Không and Jina van Hengel). "We just stop. Our mind comes back to our body, and our mind and body become one. We stop thinking. After that, we feel new so we can look at the sky like a new sky and we look at our friend like a new friend. We start a new day."

The day I first arrived at Plum Village, tired from a three-hour train ride from Paris, I was greeted by a young Vietnamese nun with a shaved head and dark, bright eyes. She took me to the large open kitchen and served me rice, tea, and a bowl of delicious vegetable broth. "Make yourself at home," she said. When I was finished eating, the nun led me to a room that looked to have once been a barn. A wall of windows had replaced the barn door, and the floor now was covered with blonde hardwood. An upright piano stood against the wall, with a book of sheet music opened to Beethoven. Two rows of black *zafus* (meditation cushions) led to an altar, where a Buddha sat in full lotus position beneath an arrangement of wildflowers. The nun invited me to sit. Then she left.

I could feel the uplifting energy in the room. I felt myself relax, my mind slow down. Following the instructions I had read in *Being Peace*, perhaps Nhat Hanh's best-known book, I began paying attention to my breathing, the inhalations and exhalations. As I sat there I developed a deep appreciation for the sound of water running off the roof and pattering against the ground.

After about half an hour, the nun returned to take me to my room in the women's quarters. We walked through mud, grass, and stones toward a long, flat building constructed of concrete. The nun opened the door on a white room with a concrete floor and a wooden ceiling, a bed made of plywood with a foam pad. Simple and clean.

Dinner began with the rich resonance of a gong. We ate in silence, having been asked to chew each mouthful fifty times and to remain at the table for half an hour. I sat at a long table with a group of American teenage girls—on a tour of spiritually based, ecologically conscious communities in Europe, Russia, and India. Several times the teenagers, passing meaningful looks, seemed to be on the verge of exploding into laughter, but they controlled themselves. On the other side of the room, a group of thirteen Vietnamese nuns sat around a big, square table. I counted six other Western women.

Dinner was delicious—home-cooked Vietnamese dishes of vegetables from the community's autumn garden. After half an hour, a bell rang three times, signaling the end of the silent eating meditation. A burst of laughter and talking followed, as the American girls at my table spilled into animated conversations about food, tea, and boys.

I went back to my room and lay down. At 8:30 the sound of the bell called me up to the evening meditation. Walking up to the *zendo* (meditation hall), I smelled wood-burning stoves. It was a cool, foggy night. Wind rattled the leaves. In the distance, the lights went off in a church on the hill.

We sat for twenty minutes. A bell rang, then we walked around the zendo, our hands folded, as if in prayer. At the sound of another bell, we returned to our cushions and meditated for another twenty minutes.

Yet another bell signified the beginning of chanting. Led by one of the nuns, we invoked the name of the Bodhisattva Avalokitesvara, expressing our desire to learn his way of listening in order to help relieve the suffering in the world. We invoked the name of Manjusri, from whom we wished to learn his way of being still and looking deeply into the heart of things, into the hearts of people. We invoked the name of Samantabhadra, saying how we aspired to practice his way of acting with the eyes and heart of compassion. We vowed to bring joy to one person

---

✳ Invoking the Bodhisattvas' Names

We invoke your name, Avalokitesvara. We aspire to learn your way of listening in order to help relieve the suffering in the world. You know how to listen in order to understand. We invoke your name in order to practice listening with all our attention and openheartedness. We will sit and listen without any prejudice. We will sit and listen without judging or reacting. We will sit and listen in order to understand. We will sit and listen so attentively that we will be able to hear what the other person is saying and also what is being left unsaid. We know that just by listening deeply we already alleviate a great deal of pain and suffering in the other person.

We invoke your name, Manjusri. We aspire to learn your way, which is to be still and to look deeply into the heart of things and into the hearts of people. We will look with all our attention and openheartedness. We will look with unprejudiced eyes. We will look without judging or reacting. We will look deeply so that we will be able to see and understand the roots of ill-being, the impermanent and selfless nature of all that is. We will practice your way of using the sword of understanding to cut through the bonds of ill-being, thus freeing ourselves and other species.

We invoke your name, Samantabhadra. We aspire to practice your aspiration to act with the eyes and heart of compassion. We vow to bring joy to one person in the morning and to ease the pain of one person in the afternoon. We know that the happiness of others is our own happiness, and we vow to practice joy on the path of service. We know that every word, every look, every action, and every smile can bring happiness to others. We know that if we practice wholeheartedly, we ourselves may become an inexhaustible source of peace and joy for our loved ones and for all species.

—from *Plum Village Chanting Book*

A song precedes morning walking meditation

in the morning and to ease the pain of one person in the afternoon. We acknowledged that the happiness of others was our own happiness, and vowed to practice joy on the path of service.

After the meditation, I walked back to my room in silence, filled with the kind of simple awareness that arises out of deep silence. I'm alive, I thought, walking on this Earth. I have my eyes, which are more precious than jewels, and my ears, another set of jewels, and my health, more precious than all the riches of the world.

Sister Chân Không, now in her mid-fifties, met Nhat Hanh when she was in her early twenties and working in the slums of Saigon, helping poor people get food, medical care, and education. When she started this work, at eighteen, she was thinking of becoming a Buddhist nun. But her first Buddhist teacher tried to persuade her to study only scriptures and to cease her social work. Her work was too important to her, however, so she dropped the idea of taking her vows.

Then she met her second teacher, Nhat Hanh, who himself was involved in creating social programs for poor people. He encouraged her to continue her work. Sister Chân Không went on to become one of his senior students in the struggle to bring peace to Vietnam, to help boat people

and refugees, and to assist the oppressed in the postwar years. Five years ago she became a nun, taking her vows during a trip to India with Nhat Hanh.

When she is not serving as Nhat Hanh's assistant during his many retreats for Europeans, Americans and Vietnamese refugees, she oversees a fund-raising campaign at Plum Village to assist orphans, war victims, political prisoners in Vietnam, and refugees languishing in Southeast Asia's camps. "I write to the refugee camps," she says, "and let the people there know they are not forgotten by the human family."

One day during my stay, Sister Chân Không presented for the Western visitors a slide show depicting the plight of the refugees. She introduced it by recounting a mission that she and Nhat Hanh undertook to rescue boat people attempting to make their way to refugee camps after the war. After their first operation had rescued 588 boat people, authorities in Singapore shut it down. So Sister Chân Không and Thich Nhat Hanh started another program in Thailand. "We disguised ourselves as fishermen," Sister Chân

Không recalled. "We had a big boat and a small boat. When we saw a refugee boat, we put our small boat into the sea and went to them. We could not take them in our boat. We only gave them a compass because they were lost in the sea. They didn't know where to go. We said that if you go in that direction you'll reach a refugee camp in Thailand and they'll accept you. If you reach another province nearby, they'll chase you away."

The slide presentation was a disturbing sequence of pictures of Vietnamese families locked behind barbed wire fences—people whom Sister Chân Không described as having been doctors, lawyers, engineers in their native land. As one upsetting image faded into the next, I noticed myself growing tense. "Breathing in, I am space," I told myself, reciting from a Nhat Hanh poem. "Breathing out, I am free." As my breathing brought relief, I understood the connection in Nhat Hanh's work between meditation and social activism. Strengthened by my own breath, I turned my attention back to a slide of a Vietnamese child who had lost her parents, sisters, brothers, uncles, and aunts during the escape from Vietnam to Thailand. "When you have a big pain you don't know how to resolve," Sister Chân Không was saying, "go back to your breath."

Watching one's breath is a tenet of any meditation center. The approach at Plum Village, however, exemplifies Nhat Hanh's unconventional practice of the traditionally austere and serious Zen. When students hear a mindfulness bell, for example, Nhat Hanh instructs them to breathe in and out consciously at least three times, then smile lightly to acknowledge the peace and joy and to witness that the practice is not such a solemn thing.

The melting away of solemnity characterizes the spirituality of Plum Village. Nhat Hanh tells visitors that they should not be uncomfortable during meditation. If their legs go to sleep, they should move. The point of meditation is not to suffer, he says, but to feel calm in the present moment. "We have to be in this life of suffering in order to transform our point of view," Nhat Hanh says. "If we live in this world and see that everything is wonderful, including our suffering, we are free."

Freedom of spirit is a part of daily life in this little community in the French countryside. At Nhat Hanh's twice-weekly talks about Buddhist sutras and thought, children over the age of six are encouraged to participate. At afternoon tea ceremonies, nuns are urged to sing—something forbidden in Vietnamese tradition. Nhat Hanh has seen the value of creativity. His gifts as a

Rèmy

writer and thinker have enabled him to translate basic Buddhist tenets, such as "enlightened bodhisattva action," into poetry that inspires people from various traditions and cultures to reconsider their capacity to care, to reevaluate what they are contributing to the political, social, and environmental well-being of the Earth. The sweetness and sincerity of his words—no matter how disturbing the subject—transmit hope rather than despair.

Despair and Empowerment at Plum Village

At the end of a conference on "Buddhism in Action" held in Amsterdam in May 1984, the group of seventy-five attendees discussed what to do next. One of the people raised his hand and said that he thought we should be in touch with our feelings about a possible nuclear war. Thich Nhat Hanh invited him to come to the head of the room and say more on the subject. He did so, and before we knew what was happening, we were launched on a pocket version of a workshop on despair and empowerment.

It was too sudden. The Dutch are very much in touch with their feelings about war. Memories of the German occupation and the holocaust are painfully fresh. People started weeping and walking out of the meeting. I took it upon myself to intervene and told a story about Plum Village to illustrate how despair and empowerment are the same thing.

When Anne Aitken and I were visiting Plum Village before the conference, Sister Chân Không was called to the telephone at the Lower Hamlet. When she returned an hour later her face was utterly tragic, and she was in tears. It seems that their friend Doan Quoc Sy, a writer in Vietnam who had served four years in a forced labor camp from 1976 to 1980 had been arrested again, and his fate was unknown.

However, Sister Chân Không had in hand a stack of press releases about Mr. Doan's arrest, which she had typed up and reproduced in that hour in the Lower Hamlet. She had also already called Amnesty International, PEN International, and other organizations that could give help. That night, she stayed up late, not only to pack for our trip north the next day, but also to address and stamp envelopes to organizations and individuals that could be useful in effecting Mr. Doan's release.

I remarked to the conferees that I thought Sister Chân Không, Thich Nhat Hanh, and their friends at Plum Village could not be as effective as they are, as empowered in the best sense of that word, if they were not also filled with despair.

How do we use despair? The Plum Village community uses the despair that everyone there feels, and together the members inspire their friends who remain in Vietnam, their friends in the expatriate Vietnamese community, and us all.

—Robert Aitken

The Plum Village community stresses the rewards to be found in simple things: gardening, cooking, making tofu, the smile of a child, the color of the sky. Some visitors, however, have a hard time adjusting. "The conditions are so primitive here," said one man I met. "And Thây could build so many buildings from the honoraria he receives giving so many retreats, instead he sends the money to the children in Vietnam. He doesn't want fancy stuff, doesn't think it will make him happy. He's happy like this."

The gentle, humble way of Nhat Hanh can be disarming. He shifts easily from conducting serious Buddhist ritual to relaxing in a circle with community residents, sharing stories, jokes, and songs. One day during my stay he shared lunch with us. A young nun, out of respect, set a special table for him, apart from everyone else. He sat there, I guess, out of respect, too. When the silent period ended, he said in a soft voice, "I feel lonely." We all laughed, and he joined us at the big square table.

He had dinner with us that night, too. At the end of the meal, he wrote song lyrics in Vietnamese and English on a blackboard and taught us how to sing the song in Vietnamese, as only three Westerners were in the room. Everyone giggled as he encouraged the nuns to try. They sang, one by one, each voice a different offering. After much prodding by the nuns at my side, I sang a solo. At the end everyone laughed, amazed at the strange sound of my first Vietnamese.

One afternoon, as the others follow Nhat Hanh down a muddy path into the woods for a walking meditation, I stay with Sister Chân Không. She has arranged for me to meet with Nhat Hanh later in the day, so I have asked her to tell me more about him and about Plum Village.

We sit by a wood stove, and she tells me the story of Claude Thomas, an American Vietnam veteran who came to the community. Deeply disturbed by his experiences in the war, the man upon his arrival seemed to be afraid that Nhat Hanh or Sister Chân Không would try to ambush him—set mines in the community's paths and fields—in revenge for his killing their countrymen. He pitched his tent off the property, in the woods. Gradually, as the community welcomed him into the fold, he came closer. "To be able to feel accepted in a community of Vietnamese people and to be able to work with them," says Sister Chân Không, "for him was a wonderful feeling."

Chân Không also recalls for me her experiences accompanying Thich Nhat Hanh at Vietnam vet-

Lantern-making for the Hiroshima Day ceremony

erans' retreats in the United States. "When they come together in a group like that, the atmosphere is so heavy, and they only have five days to resolve many problems," she says. "One man had killed so many Vietnamese children during the war, he couldn't stand to be in a room with any children. Thây told him, 'You may have killed children in the past, but you can save children's lives in the present.' That was a big insight for him."

After the others return from their meditative walk, I sit and talk with an American man who has lived at Plum Village, on and off, for three years. "This isn't utopia," says Scott Mayer, a forty-three-year-old from Portland, Oregon. "It's the real world, and here we have all the problems that are everywhere else. Thây tries to teach us how to deal with these difficulties."

As Scott talks, I review in my mind the list of criticisms that people have taken me aside to express. So much money goes to assisting orphans, political dissidents, and refugees, one person

complained to me, that the community itself sometimes lacks funds. At times, said another person, it seems like the right hand doesn't know what the left hand is doing at Plum Village; for example, it's hard to get information about Nhat Hanh's schedule. That these people felt comfortable telling a journalist that their community isn't perfect impressed me. It meant that they feel free. It meant that the community could handle real people, real lives, problems, dissent.

I also reflect back on a conversation that I had with a Vietnamese couple from Texas, here for a two-week stay. The husband had spent four painful years in Communist reeducation camps in Vietnam before escaping by boat to a refugee camp, and eventually winning permission to move to the United States. He said he had known of Nhat Hanh since he was seventeen. "Thây was brilliant, always coming up with new ideas, always a rebel," the man recalled. "A rebel in the sense that he said Buddhism had to be fresh and meaningful for the people of whatever culture it touched: French Buddhism in France, American Buddhism in America, and Indian Buddhism in India. A lot of people in Vietnam were against Thây. They didn't want Buddhism to be new. They wanted it to remain as it had been, and Thây was changing it."

My mind shifts to the story of another visitor I met, a twenty-nine-year-old Bostonian. During a community gathering he told us about his upcoming peace pilgrimage—a ten month, 3,000-mile walk from Panama to Washington to honor indigenous peoples and protest celebrations surrounding the anniversary of Columbus' discovery of America. "Please practice mindfulness as you walk," I remember Chân Không responding. "That way you will bring peace to yourself and peace to the Earth. You will be in touch with the Earth and the whole universe around you. Your strongest aims are in the ground of your being, but if your mind is not peaceful, you cannot realize them." With this thought fresh in my mind, I start across the field for my appointment with Nhat Hanh. Sister Chân Không is coming out of the door of his cabin with one of the young nuns. "Only a half-hour," she says.

Thây and Arnie enjoy some fresh plums

"Okay," I say with a nod. "A half-hour." A half-hour with a Zen master seems a luxury.

As I enter his room, Nhat Hanh greets me like a warm host. "How is your stay here? Are you enjoying Plum Village?" He offers me a seat on a meditation cushion on the floor at a low table. Before sitting I glance around the room, at his bookcase, desk, and assorted shelves. Noticing my interest, Nhat Hanh directs me to a picture sitting on a shelf, amid his books. It shows him as a new monk, at sixteen. "Oh, goodness," I say. "You look like a child!"

"Every time I see that photograph," he says, "I have compassion for the young boy." He pauses, pouring some tea. "Enjoying your stay?"

"Yes, very much," I respond, feeling at home in his quiet place. I turn on my tape recorder to start the interview. We begin by talking about the increasing awareness among Americans about protecting the environment and their own personal health. From there, our discussion glides easily

toward the need to refrain from ingesting toxins, to developing compassion, to stopping war before it ever starts. We talk about children and the importance of their role in a spiritual community. "When children are happy," the smiling monk says to me, "adults can be happy too."

It is a conversation that could go on for hours. After a while, I look at my watch and notice that we have been talking for nearly a half-hour. "I see that our time is running out," I begin, "so, last question…"

A soft laugh comes from Nhat Hanh. "Time is there. It does not run. You are the one who runs." It is so quiet, so peaceful in his room that I can hear his breath. "Drink your tea," he says, smiling at me as if to acknowledge how wonderful stillness is. He picks up the pot and refills my cup. "Don't hurry."

Plum Village Summer Opening

Anne Cushman

Vietnamese Zen master Thich Nhat Hanh's meditation community in the south of France is an abode of harmony, peace, and ethnic diversity. As I drive past the vineyards, chateaux, and sunflower fields of southwestern France, en route to Plum Village, I find myself wondering why I'm going there for my vacation. Wouldn't I really rather be exploring the nearby medieval town of St. Emilion, famous for its macaroons? Or sampling Bordeaux wines? Or slathering Camembert onto French bread while lounging on a beach? But after five minutes in Plum Village, all doubts vanish. This is clearly not a monastery—children race about laughing and calling to each other in Vietnamese, French, and English; gray-haired women chatter in Vietnamese as they prepare rice and vegetables in the communal kitchen; a group of teenagers sit under a tree playing sitars. But permeating all this activity is a sense of peace and simplicity that I find deeply refreshing after a week of frenzied tourism.

My introduction to the spirit of this unique practice center comes as I'm signing in. When the office telephone rings, no one jumps to answer it. Instead, everyone within earshot—children, monks, nuns, visitors from around the world—stop moving, stop talking, smile, and take three deep, slow breaths. Only then does the office manager pick up the receiver. Vietnamese Zen teacher Thich Nhat Hanh, founder of Plum Village, permitted the installation of a telephone only on the condition that it be treated this way—as one of the many "mindfulness bells" that ring throughout the day to remind practitioners to return their joyful attention to the present moment. During silent meals, a small bell invites mindfulness every few mouthfuls; in daily Dharma talks, a large bowl-shaped bell periodically reminds teacher and students to stop talking and breathe; gongs ring out over the plum orchards to call practitioners to meditation, tea ceremonies, and festivals. After several days of pausing for these bells, even digital watch alarms and distant car horns start to seem part of the chorus.

This interweaving of practice and daily living is the essence of Plum Village, founded in the early 1980s to fulfill Nhat Hanh's decades-old dream of a community where people involved in the work of social transformation could come for rest and spiritual nourishment. Exiled from his native

Walking meditation path

Vietnam because of his antiwar activities, he finally established his spiritual oasis on eighty acres of land in the wine country east of Bordeaux. In exchange for a home, Vietnamese refugees helped clean and renovate the beautiful, rustic, eighteenth-century stone farm buildings and construct additional cinder block structures. Currently, only about fifty residents stay year-round, studying Buddhism, working to help Vietnamese refugees and political prisoners, and tending the 1,250 plum trees, whose crop earns money to send medicine to Vietnam. But for one month each summer, the community is open to the public, and nearly 1,000 visitors—about half Vietnamese and half Westerners—come to practice. This month is by no means a grueling meditation retreat. In fact, Nhat Hanh likes to use the word "treat," rather than "retreat," to describe these gatherings of Buddhist practitioners. The emphasis is on learning skills for bringing mindfulness into everyday life. Family practice is central, and children are wholeheartedly encouraged to participate in all activities, including meditation, tea ceremonies, and Dharma talks. Typically, Thây directs the first ten minutes of every talk to the children, who then play outside for the rest of the talk.

This emphasis on family practice creates a unique atmosphere at Plum Village—a curious fusion of monastery and summer camp. One evening, for example, we are guided through a version of the classic Buddhist meditation on impermanence and death. While we sit in half lotus and visualize our loved ones' bodies turning purple, rotting, and disintegrating, we can hear the happy shrieks of children playing volleyball outside the meditation hall. The daily schedule at Plum Village begins and ends with seated meditation. Daily Dharma talks by Nhat Hanh alternate among English, French, and Vietnamese, and are simultaneously translated through headphones into at least the other two languages, and some-

times German, Italian, and Russian as well. Each day Nhat Hanh also leads walking meditation, a slow, silent excursion through the orchards, fields, and woods, past magnificent vistas of rolling hills and golden acres of sunflowers. During my visit, we often pause in a clearing during walking meditation to sing songs in French, English, and Vietnamese, about how wonderful it is to breathe, smile, and walk.

One of the missions of Plum Village is to help exiled Vietnamese families keep their cultural legacy alive as well as share it with Westerners. Frequent performances, festivals, and ceremonies celebrate the Vietnamese heritage. One day, the children make star-shaped lanterns out of bamboo and brightly colored tissue paper to celebrate the Full Moon Festival. Another evening, teenagers perform traditional Vietnamese music and dance.

Accommodations are spartan—shared dormitory rooms with bare walls and narrow cots—and many visitors choose instead to pitch their own tents on the property. Practitioners are asked to participate in daily chores, including cleaning, gardening, and helping to prepare the communal vegetarian meals. However, ample time is allotted for relaxation, making friends, quiet contemplation—and even an occasional outing to a nearby lake.

No matter what the activity, visitors are gently reminded to perform it with joy and awareness. For me, the spirit of Plum Village is epitomized by the carved wooden sign beside the walking meditation path: "The mind can go in a thousand directions, but on this beautiful path, I walk in peace. With each step, a gentle wind blows. With each step, a flower blooms."

Spring in Plum Village

Thomas C. Fox

S hortly after noon on a sunny day in May of last year, I purchased a 61 franc ($12) ticket at the Bordeaux train depot and set off east to a small town called Ste. Foy La Grande, an hour away. Ste. Foy was the tiniest of dots on my tourist map and the last verification I was nearing my destination— Plum Village, the home of a small community of Vietnamese and Western Buddhists headed by Vietnamese Zen master Thich Nhat Hanh.

Still Water Meditation Hall, in the Upper Hamlet

I first heard of Thich Nhat Hanh in 1966, shortly after I had arrived in Vietnam to work with war refugees as a volunteer for International Voluntary Services, a private relief organization. Nhat Hanh's pacifist writings were, at the time, capturing the imagination of many war-sickened Vietnamese, especially the young, and specifically university students in Saigon, where two years earlier he, along with a group of university professors and students, had founded the School of Youth for Social Service.

At the time, talk of being peaceful one step at a time, reconciling with one's enemies, and working to serve others seemed innocuous enough. But Nhat Hanh and his followers were viewed as a threat by South Vietnam government officials. They suspected virtually any Buddhist intention at the time. Not long after that, the monk's writings were banned and he was no longer welcome in his native land. A quarter century of exile was about to begin. Curiously, when the Communists took over in 1975 they, too, found no comfort in Nhat Hanh's brand of pacifism and would not allow him to return to Vietnam. The Zen master's path eschews political ideologies of all stripes.

As the war spread during the tumultuous 1960s, so, too, did word in the United States of the unusual Vietnamese Buddhist who opposed the conflict and seemed to embody the aspirations of war-weary Vietnamese. Nhat Hanh's views began to be picked up by U.S. peace activists, and, in 1966, he accepted an invitation from Fellowship of Reconciliation, a religion-

based peace organization, to come to the U.S.
Nhat Hanh, Buddhist peace ambassador, was one
of the few prominent Vietnamese who could call
for an end to the conflict without being cast as a
communist. During this journey, he may have
altered U.S. history when he met Martin Luther
King, Jr. He so impressed the civil rights leader
that King called a press conference in Chicago
and, with Nhat Hanh at his side, declared for the
first time his opposition to the Vietnam War. That
announcement marked the wedding of two focus-
es of U.S. unrest at the time, the civil rights and
antiwar movements. The marriage eventually top-
pled President Johnson and helped shape a gener-
ation of young idealists. A year later, King, the
1964 Nobel Peace Prize laureate, nominated
Nhat Hanh for the 1967 prize, writing, "[He]
offers a way out of this nightmare, a solution
acceptable to rational leaders.... His ideas for
peace, if applied, would build a momentum to
ecumenism, to world brotherhood, to humanity."

In May 1966, Nhat Hanh also visited Trappist
monk Thomas Merton at Gethsemani, near
Louisville, Kentucky, and made another lasting
impression. Speaking of Nhat Hanh, Merton said
to his student novices, "Just the way he opens the
door and enters a room, he demonstrates his
understanding. He is a true monk." Following the
visit, Merton wrote in *Jubilee* magazine (August
1966), "[Nhat Hanh] represents the young, the
defenseless, the new ranks of youth who find
themselves with every hand turned against them
except those of the peasants and the poor, with
whom they are working. Nhat Hanh speaks truly
for the people of Vietnam.... Nhat Hanh is my
brother."

After leaving the United States, Nhat Hanh
went to Europe where he had an audience with
Pope Paul VI. The two religious figures urged
greater cooperation between Catholics and
Buddhists to help bring peace to Vietnam.

Brothers Gary and Phâp Dâng shop for produce in Bergerac

I met Nhat Hanh two years after that, in May
of 1968, when we were both in Paris for the
opening of the peace talks to end the Vietnam
War. We spent an afternoon together talking
about Vietnam and the prospects for peace. A
year later, at the request of the Unified Buddhist
Church of Vietnam, Nhat Hanh headed up the
Buddhist Peace Delegation at the ongoing talks.
Accords were finally signed in 1973, but Nhat
Hanh was told he could not return to Vietnam.
His exile was taking on a permanent look. One
door closed so he opened another, establishing a
small Buddhist community one hundred miles
southwest of Paris. That community moved to
Plum Village in 1982.

I was reflecting on those early years when the
train pulled into Ste. Foy La Grande. The depot's
sole ticket agent was asleep behind a glass parti-
tion, so I walked across the street to a café, and

asked someone to call a taxi, one of the town's handful. The driver said he knew where the Buddhists were living about eight miles out of town, and soon we were winding our way along a two-lane asphalt road to Plum Village.

The village—actually two "hamlets," one for men, the other for women during the wintertime—is comprised of a half dozen nineteenth-century stone farmhouses converted into dormitories. Each hamlet has kitchens and dining halls with concrete floors, and meditation halls—large, open rooms with glass windows, and smooth, wooden floors adorned with cloth cushions and straw mats. On the walls hang simple brush drawings. Buddha statues sitting on simple altars provide prayerful focal points.

As I arrived, three elderly women wearing gray robes and stooping in a small garden stopped planting vegetable seeds to look up at me. I was greeted by a wide-smiling, thirtyish-looking Western monk who identified himself as Brother Gary. Slenderly built in his monk's robe, this man from Houston, Texas, had been appointed to be my personal host. Later, Brother Gary explained that people from all over the world come to Plum Village to practice mindfulness, some for a week and some for months at a time. Nhat Hanh and the two dozen other permanent residents run Plum Village as a retreat center for Vietnamese, Europeans and others from as far away as North America and Asia.

During my brief stay, community members were preparing for the Summer Opening, the peak traffic period from mid-July to mid-August. Several monks were washing sleeping bags in buckets of water and stomping them with their bare feet in much the way select wines are produced in the Bordeaux region.

That afternoon, Brother Gary and I sat down in the shade of a tree not far from a bamboo rock garden. As we talked, a monk struck a brass gong

❋
Sangha Building in Texas

I have read many of Thây's books since a friend gave me a copy of Being Peace *in 1990, and I attended a wonderful retreat with Thây and the community in West Virginia in September 1993. This has all had a profound influence on my life and ministry as a Catholic priest.*

I live in a part of the United States where there is a growing Mexican population and growing violence due to despair. We do not have some of the problems of major U.S. cities yet—there is a lot of goodness and generosity. Still, the despair in young people grows, and we are beginning to see gangs developing. My parish is active in these social issues and has succeeded to some extent in increasing hope in our community.

We are experimenting with ways of making Eucharist like tea meditation, so as to deepen our experience of community and friendship. We sometimes do meditation on emptiness as part of the Eucharistic celebration. We talk about Eucharist as saying "yes" and "thanks" to Life. We also see in the wheat and grapes our solidarity with farming and Third World peoples. We see blood and sweat, aching backs, and assassinations in what we call the "Body and Blood of Christ." We see our connectedness and deepen our love for each other.

Meditation and the many other forms of mindfulness development Thây teaches have been of tremendous help to me. They are in deep communion with our Western Catholic mystical tradition, yet the beautiful articulation of them in the Zen tradition enriches our own spiritual lineage. Thây's teaching, a wonderful bridge between East and West, has also helped me deal with anger and depression. I have grown to appreciate rather than resent some of our family's struggles over the years.

When I returned to the Rio Grande last September following the retreat, I shared with some friends about mindfulness. Some were already familiar with Thây's writing. Since then we have built a small Sangha—practicing sitting and walking meditation, tea celebration, and precepts recitations.

—Mark Matthews, S.M.

TIẾNG CHUÔNG CHÙA CỔ

(The Temple Bell on Top of the Mountain)

Tuoi, khoe

Thich Nhat Hanh

Ba nghiệp lắng thanh tịnh gửi lòng theo tiếng chuông Nguyện người nghe tỉnh thức, vượt thoát nẻo đau buồn. Boong boong. Tôi là chuông đại hồng ngôi chùa xưa trên đỉnh núi.... Boong boong Tôi khua vang mở đầu cho một bình minh mới... Boong boong Nghe tiếng

hanging from a tree nearby. (The Buddhists actually don't say "hit" or "struck." They say "invited the bell to sound.") The strokes were slow and deliberate, and all in earshot stopped their work and stood still. I looked to Brother Gary, who had stopped talking in mid-sentence and closed his eyes. With a slight smile on his lips, he took a deep breath, exhaled, then took another. We were in the midst of a fifteen-to-twenty-second breathing meditation. Brother Gary explained that at the sound of any bell—the community gong, a distant church bell, a chime clock, or even the ring of a telephone—community members stop and practice mindful breathing. Bells, he told me, "are invited to return the community to awareness. Breathing is the key to mindfulness." He said I needed to breathe consciously and recognize my breath as a contact point with the air around me, and, in a wider sense, all life that has been, is, and will be on Earth. "When your mind is attentive to all this, you are also in contact with your mind," he added. The habit of mindfulness, he said, creates an awareness of the singular beauty of the moment—the "eternal now." This

tôi xin người nở nụ cười Boong boong Nghe tiếng

tôi xin người đem mắt thương nhìn cuộc đời. Boong

boong thở.... vào tâm người tỉnh lặng Boong boong Thở

ra miệng người mím cười Boong boong Người trở

về phút giây hiện tại. Boong boong Người an

trú phút giây tuyệt vời.

awareness helps overcome suffering. "It has helped me realize, for example, even when I am hurting for one reason or another that I am more than my suffering." My mind lingered on Gary's last thought as the gong tolled again, calling us to eat.

We lined up single file in the dining hall, in silence, and it reminded me of other visits to monastic dining halls or retreats. Then we served ourselves, scooping vegetable stew out of a large pot with metal ladles. Simple food. No one spoke during the first twenty minutes of the meal. This is when the community "eats in mindfulness." A brochure explained it this way: "To eat in mind-

fulness is of great spiritual benefit and of great benefit to our physical health. It is being aware of what you are chewing and not letting your mind be occupied by anything else....Chew every mouthful at least fifty times [in gratitude and an awareness of the interbeing of all things]."

Fifty times? I tried, but even at thirty my pace had slowed almost beyond tolerance. "Mindfulness," I realized, had something to offer me. A challenge, another perspective on life. After twenty minutes a small bell was invited three times, and conversations commenced. A woman asked

A novice monk floats like a cloud, enjoying free time in the Upper Hamlet

Breathing in, I know I am breathing in.
Breathing out, I know I am breathing out.
Breathing in, I see myself as a flower.
Breathing out, I feel fresh.
Breathing in, I see myself as a mountain.
Breathing out, I feel solid.
Breathing in, I see myself as still water.
Breathing out, I reflect things as they are.
Breathing in, I see myself as space.
Breathing out, I feel free.

The monks at Plum Village recite gathas throughout the day—when waking up, during meals, while walking or doing common chores, and at other key moments. There seem to be an infinite variety of gathas, all aimed at focusing the mind, connecting the simple with the profound. During meditation that evening, I was told not only to be conscious of my breathing, but to enjoy it. The exercise lasted for some twenty minutes. Then the monks stood up and began a "walking meditation," inhaling with each left step, exhaling with each right step. After that, it was twenty more minutes of breathing meditation before ending the service with Buddhist chants.

It was time to retire. My psyche had slowed substantially, but to really "come down," I had been told, would take at least several days. Already I felt myself entering a space where I began to pay more attention to ordinary things. The wooden door, the green plant on the table, the spiderweb in a corner of the room. I thought of a passage I had read in *Being Peace*: "To meditate is to be aware of what is going on—in our bodies, our feelings, our minds, and in the world. When we settle in the present moment, we can see beauties and wonders right before our eyes." The moon was bright and full that night, framed by the single window in my room. I looked out, drifting into sleep thinking of how contemplative life envelops all religious traditions, and I felt a surge of gratitude.

A Dharma, or teaching, talk is a Buddhist tradition and an important twice-weekly event at the village. One was scheduled the next day. Nhat Hanh was to speak on mindfulness and its applications in Vietnamese poetry. We gathered in the

me in English (we spoke in English and Vietnamese) what the Catholic church's attitude was toward Buddhism. I assured her, perhaps overstating the case, that my church was very open to other religions and wanted to learn from them.

That evening, the gong sounded and it was time for evening meditation. By then, the women had returned to their hamlet—celibacy is taught for monastics as a requisite path to inner freedom—and we were moving toward the meditation center. I was invited to sit on a cushion in a full or half-lotus position if I could and, if not, then to kneel on a small wooden bench, tucking my legs beneath me. Again I was to breathe consciously and slowly, repeat a gatha:

men's dining room and the monk spoke for close to two hours. One Buddhist woman whispered simultaneous translations to the non-Vietnamese-speaking visitors.

The poem, *The Tale of Kieu*, is about a Vietnamese woman sold into prostitution to earn her family's liberation. Nhat Hanh spoke of Vietnam's self-imposed slavery to capitalism and communism, suggesting that Vietnam will not be free until it develops a deeper self-awareness. "Mindfulness," he argued, "is the path to that awareness."

Following the talk, twenty of us walked mindfully with Nhat Hanh to his hut, a one-room wooden structure on the side of a hill overlooking a green meadow. The room was barren except for a low table behind which the monk sat in a lotus position after we entered. I sat down on the floor, waiting for someone to speak, but there was only silence—for more than fifteen minutes. Then Nhat Hanh nodded and the visitors began to get up to leave.

That afternoon I returned to the monk's hut for a personal visit. He greeted me with a smile, inviting me to sit down next to him at the table on the floor. But now on the table sat an old thermos and two small glasses with straw coasters beneath them. He poured tea and asked the first question, "How are Vietnamese refugees faring in the United States?"

I answered that Vietnamese in the United States generally have a reputation for being industrious and most have found some kind of employment. But that was not what he was asking. He said he wanted to know how they were handling the separation from their homeland. He especially wanted to know about the young. He had heard that many young people were estranged from their parents and some had joined gangs. Additionally, he wanted to know what the Catholic Church was doing to reach the young. "What authentic Catholic teaching," he asked, "is speaking to the alienated young?"

As I struggled to capture the full gist of his probe, he continued, saying that Western church leaders need to work harder to reach the young. He said it was his impression that material things, like designer clothes and fast music, were filling needs that were not being met by religious teach-

---

❋

The Refuge Chant

At the foot of the Bodhi tree,
beautifully seated, peaceful and smiling,
the living source of understanding and compassion,
to the Buddha I go for refuge.

The path of mindful living,
leading to healing, joy, and enlightenment,
the way of peace,
to the Dharma I go for refuge.

The loving and supportive community of practice,
realizing harmony, awareness, and liberation,
to the Sangha I go for refuge.

I am aware that the three gems are within my heart.
I vow to realize them.
I vow to practice mindful breathing and smiling,
looking deeply into things.
I vow to understand living beings and their suffering,
to cultivate compassion and loving kindness,
and to practice joy and equanimity.

I vow to offer joy to one person in the morning
and to help relieve the grief of one person
in the afternoon.
I vow to live simply and sanely, content with just a few
possessions,
and to keep my body healthy.
I vow to let go of all worries and anxiety
in order to be light and free.

I am aware that I owe so much to my parents,
teachers, friends, and all beings.
I vow to be worthy of their trust,
to practice wholeheartedly,
so that understanding and compassion will flower,
and I can help living beings be free from their suffering.
May the Buddha, the Dharma, and the Sangha
support my efforts.

—from *Plum Village Chanting Book*

ers. He quickly added that Buddhism is not the answer to America's search for meaning. "That answer," he said, "must come from within Western traditions. At best, Buddhism can help point the way." He stressed that Catholic leaders,

Photo of Thich Nhat Hanh as a 16-year-old novice

including Catholic journalists, need to search the Catholic tradition for "authentic teachings" capable of reaching the young. "It must be authentic in order to be heard," he said, adding that by authentic he means teachings grounded in "true understanding and true love." He felt the Catholic Church's leadership was preoccupied with the wrong concerns, but he would not spell them out except to cite the examples of birth control and church authority. Vietnamese Buddhism avoids dogmatism. The first precept of Thich Nhat Hanh's Order of Interbeing reads, "Do not be idolatrous about or bound to any doctrine, theory, or ideology, even Buddhist ones. Buddhist systems of thought are guiding means; they are not absolute truth."

We spoke of Vietnam, and I asked if he would like to return. He said he has never stopped wanting to return but has grown to realize that as long as he has followers there, "I am in Vietnam." Clearly, his exile has been painful, but he has adjusted to it. He spoke of Buddhism's Four Noble Truths: the recognition of suffering, the isolation of its cause, the healing and the rooting out of the cause, and the path to liberation. This process, he said, has helped him deal with personal suffering and opened his eyes to the world's beauty in the midst of suffering. "Removing the cause of the suffering," he said, "opens us up to the presence of the Kingdom of God. It is the recognition that the Kingdom is available here and now. St. Francis understood this." And he told the story about Francis asking a tree to talk about God's presence. The tree responded, so the story goes, by blooming in midwinter.

We lingered over tea for more than an hour. Nhat Hanh has written that through our attitude we can do violence to tea, just as we can to anything else. Violence is an attitude, and each personal act—because all is interconnected—is part of the quest for universal peace. It came to me as we spoke, that this unassuming monk, exiled from his land and dismissed by the secular powers that be, was, indeed, the genuine thing. Martin Luther King, Jr. recognized it; so did Thomas Merton. Sitting there that afternoon, with a small glass of tea in hand, looking into Thich Nhat Hanh's clear brown eyes, I felt the presence of a holy man—and, through him, felt connected in a special way with those spiritual giants. Truth's pathway can, in rare moments, appear so clear, so simple.

Plum Village—A Place for Children

Michele Hill

This summer I traveled halfway around the world, from Hawaii to France, to participate in the simple retreat life of Plum Village. Like many others before me, I traveled far only to meet myself. Dropping my busy mind from the trip and my life, I realized how much I miss by rushing ahead of myself. Each day I settled into the rhythm of Plum Village, slowing down my walking, eating, talking, and I noticed newcomers experiencing the same feelings. My bowing and smiling increased as the days passed and I experienced a joyful feeling of connection to everything around me—people, animals, flowers, stars and myself. I laughed when one of the first things I heard Thich Nhat Hanh say after I arrived was, "Going a long way looking for a teacher is like chasing clouds. A leaf can be a teacher, or a tree, or a person...you are your own teacher."

Others have written about this very special community, established by the monk who has become a leader not only for Vietnamese Buddhists, but Western students of mindfulness and meditation practice. Originally begun for Vietnamese refugees in Europe, now there are people from all over northern Europe, the United States, and even from Sri Lanka and Bangladesh, staying during the summer retreat month and following as little or as much of the schedule as they choose. Despite a variety of languages and practice backgrounds, there develops quite quickly a shared purpose and a true spirit of community as people live and work together in the two hamlets of Plum Village surrounded by vineyards, sunflowers, and the exquisite peacefulness of the old French countryside.

Melodie putting on her shoes outside the meditation hall

Perhaps the most impressive thing to me—and the one I wish to write about here—was the place of children at Plum Village.

The kind of Zen practice that many of us have practiced over the last decade or so in the West has essentially been that of a modified monastic schedule. Rarely, if ever, have we had visitors with children come to an entire training period. And those who may have come for a brief visit have had to rely on their own resources to deal with the issue of childcare, often sharing with other parents.

As more of our Sangha members have had children, the separation between a lay, family life and this essentially monastic practice has increased dramatically. This separation has been felt not only by parents, but by the community as a whole. In many cases the participation and input of several of the oldest Zen students among us have been lost. When I left for Plum Village this summer, this dilemma remained unresolved.

But at Plum Village I found that children are not only present, they are the center of the community. They participate in everything and people pay attention to them quite naturally. At several group discussions, the issue of including children in practice was raised by Thây.

Thây asked for ideas from the non-Vietnamese on how to include their children, who often had more difficulty adjusting to Plum Village because they were younger, had fewer role models, or did not have any previous exposure to practice. He asked an eleven-year-old American boy his ideas. Timmy suggested that American kids are bored with meditation and don't know what it is about.

Thây teaches pebble meditation—breathe in and out and move one pebble

If they find out "what's in it for them" they sit still more and are more involved. He said kids should be built up slowly to sit first for three minutes, then five minutes until they can do a whole period (at Plum Village the sitting periods are only twenty minutes), and at first the children should sit for only as long as they want to. The Vietnamese children are introduced to meditation in this way and older children show younger children what to do, becoming teachers along with everyone else in the community.

At another discussion conducted in French, Thây talked with European children and explained that practice is not just sitting. Meditation is being aware and can be something very nice. If you watch TV and eat at the same time, you miss the food and the TV. Families can see each other at dinner, he said, and so it is nice to eat in silence sometimes so we can see the ones we love—that is meditation.

At Plum Village I sat with children for the first time, and I found I enjoyed it very much. There were smiling faces next to me, looking up at me—a wonderful connection. One day two Vietnamese children and I had been playing at teaching one another songs, and when the bell rang for meditation we all went together to the zendo. I filed behind a five-year-old in *kinhin* (walking meditation) into the zendo. The experience touched the child in me.

Thây said that if you cannot explain what you are doing to your children, maybe it isn't real. Children must be included and understand what you are doing if it is to be real Buddhism. He feels that children can understand the most profound Buddhist ideas, which at the core are very simple and straightforward. As examples of this, Thây used, "You are me and I am you"; "to understand is to love—they are not separate"; and "when a finger is hurt, the whole hand suffers."

"We have to find a practice that is pleasant for children. It is very important, for if we can't include the children it is a defect. When children are included, practice will be pleasant for the parents as well," said Thây.

These words made a deep impression on me. How often I had heard my friends express feelings of being torn between being with their children and going to the zendo. Working parents whose jobs take them away from home so much are reluctant to leave their children again in the

Full Moon Festival—when the sun sets, the children light their lantern candles and walk mindfully through the Lower Hamlet

evenings or on weekends. I have noticed that while a few families in our Sangha have tried, most have abandoned the effort. It seems to me that creating a practice that can include children will solve a multitude of problems and enrich the experience for all of us.

Said Thây, "Practice is impossible without the support of children. Without this, it is an escape from family and society."

At Plum Village, there were many excellent ideas about how to include children in practice as well as explain practice to them in a way they can understand. I once heard Thây tell a story of how he explained meditation to a child using the analogy of cloudy apple juice, which was offered to a child who refused it. When the juice sat for awhile it became clear, and the child wanted to drink it. Thây told the child that if you stay quiet, you become clear like the apple juice.

Sister Chân Không explained walking meditation to a Swiss child who was having a difficult time slowing down. She asked him if he liked to be hit hard and roughly or touched gently and lovingly. When he answered the latter she said that the earth, too, likes this. So when we walk on the earth we walk as though our feet are touching the earth gently and lovingly.

Other ideas for conveying practice to children include involving them by counting to ten together, practicing with a poem, listening with them, singing and having fun together, and above all, treating them with respect and their efforts at participating with appreciation.

Children seem to have a natural love of ceremonies, rituals, songs, and games. Friends with small children have often told me that it is the child who remembers to hold hands before dinner, who seems to recognize the beauty of a small ritual like bowing on entering the meditation hall. At Plum Village, children are given regular responsibilities in the zendo, like ringing bells, leading tea meditation, and participating in ceremonies.

In addition, two times a week while I was there, children's performances were scheduled. Children were the center of these evenings. I often saw small groups of Vietnamese children practicing songs and dances during the day. Children were also involved in walking meditation. Many people walked with a child on either side holding hands. Some children walked the whole time, and others ran off to play after several minutes.

While some Sanghas in the West have experimented with many of these same ideas, there was a profound difference at Plum Village. The inclusion of the children was not "tacked on" to anything else. There wasn't "real practice" and "family practice." At Plum Village, the ideal of

Julia taking a nap in Transformation Hall

life and practice outside of the zendo was becoming a reality. The doors of the zendo have been thrown open to the laughter of children and adults, and, as a consequence, our lives were thrown open to practice in a way I did not before think possible.

Sanghas may need to look carefully at this way of Zen practice, because so many of us do not remain "monks"—unattached and with few work or family responsibilities throughout our lives.

Monastic Zen practice may work for some of us at certain times in our lives—but it has a limited value for a father, mother, or "auntie" who want to show a young child that our lives are made up of silence as well as noise. It takes away from nothing, but instead adds an important element for all of us. This is not just providing childcare so parents can "sit." It means creating situations where children can participate fully. It may mean changing the emphasis of our practice.

We have already seen many changes in the form of Buddhism as it adapts to the West. Some of these changes have come about because of the equal participation of women, and have included the elimination of sexist language, and leadership roles accessible to women. The next challenge, as I see it, is to include children. Our children will teach us how to do this naturally. The first step is to invite them in.

Soon after I returned from Plum Village, several people in my Sangha began to sit once a week in each other's houses, usually with two or three children. After only three weeks, the children have come to acknowledge this quiet meditation as something that we all do together. They enjoy lighting the incense, ringing a bell, and blowing out the candles. They drift in and out of the living room where people are sitting on their zafus facing inward in a circle. The two-year-old comes in briefly to stand silently beside her mother, with a hand on her shoulder, and then runs off to join her friend in play once again.

For us it is only a first step, but one that has been embraced with excitement, joy, and a rediscovery of something that many of us had lost.

Starting Plum Village

Chân Không

In 1971, I visited a community of peace work-ers at Auvergne and was reminded of our School of Youth for Social Service garden in Vietnam. It was wonderful to see the fields of pumpkins, cucumbers, and lettuce, but it made me sad to think of Thây in Paris taking care of one pot of mint and one pot of violet leaves on his windowsill. Every three months, he would change the soil using the little bags of earth from the market. While I was in Auvergne, I learned that French farmers were selling land and dilapi-dated farm buildings for next to nothing, so when I returned to Paris, I discussed with Thây the pos-sibility of finding a country retreat.

We looked at many places, and Thây fell in love with a tiny, old house outside the town of Fontvannes, 150 kilometers southeast of Paris. The price was $3,700. All around us were hills, meadows, and fields of wheat and corn. Although the rooms were uninhabitable—there were no doors or windows, just a chimney for burning wood and two small holes in the stone walls— Thây really wanted to buy it, so we did.

Every weekend we went from Paris to Fontvannes and began rebuilding the house. The first evening that we stayed overnight was in November, and the house was like a refrigerator. We burned dozens of logs, but it was not possible to heat the indoors. Our friend Hoang Anh and I did jumping exercises and ran outside as fast as we could, but we could not keep warm. Finally, Thây, Hoang Anh, and I spent the night on wooden planks in front of the fireplace, and Thây caught a cold.

Friends joined us each weekend to help. We constructed a bathroom and transformed the sta-ble into a warm room for Thây. The one large room became our meditation hall and living

Harvest time at the Sweet Potato Community in Fontvannes

room, and at night, the men stayed there, while the women stayed in an adjacent room. When these two rooms were too crowded, some of us slept on the kitchen floor. Every morning after sit-ting meditation, we all joined together for tea at the kitchen table, and Thây would give a Dharma talk.

By 1975, the house had become rather pleas-ant, with four rooms and a cozy kitchen, and sev-eral of us decided to move there. We named the community *Les Patates Douces* (Sweet Potatoes), because in Vietnam, sweet potatoes are the poor-est food. When peasants have no rice, they eat dried sweet potatoes, and we needed a way to feel in touch with the poorest people in our country. The communists had taken power, and we were cut off with no way to help Vietnam. I felt like a tree cut at the roots. Day after day, all I could do was follow my breathing. As I sat, walked, gardened, and cooked, I stayed aware of each breath. Every time I thought about Vietnam, I felt desperate. Thanks to that house and land, we were able to heal some of our wounds and come to appreciate the beauty of France. By this time, eleven of us lived there, and Vietnamese friends from Paris joined us on weekends.

Life in the Sweet Potato Community was meditative and joyful. We did not feel strong enough to sing traditional Vietnamese songs, so we sang songs on being in touch with the trees, the birds,

Thây and a young friend planting lettuce at the Sweet Potato Community

the sunshine, and the snow. We planted vegetables and printed books. Thây was the most skillful printer. None of us had expected him to be so adept at manual work. The Fellowship of Reconciliation gave us a Varityper, and I composed the text of *The Miracle of Mindfulness* in Vietnamese. Thây did the layout, platemaking, printing, cutting, binding, and cover design. He also wrote *The Sun My Heart*, *The History of Buddhism in Vietnam*, and many short stories. We planted lettuce, carrots, mustard greens, basil,

coriander, mint, and many Vietnamese herbs, and we discovered that Thây was also an expert gardener. He taught us how to use a hoe, dig without bending our backs too much, and aerate and cultivate the soil. In that atmosphere, I began to feel calm again.

By 1982, our Sweet Potato Community had become too small. Even with tents, we could accommodate only thirty guests, and in the summer, we often had to ask one group of thirty to leave after only a week to allow thirty more guests to come. As more and more people wanted to visit, we began looking for a new place.

Thây had heard that farmland in the south of France was cheap, and he liked the idea of living where it would be warmer and sunnier than Sweet Potato. I loved the idea of being able to grow bitter melons and Vietnamese fragrant herbs that could not withstand the cold. Our first destination was Aix-en-Provence, but when we stopped at a gas station to ask for directions, we were nearly lifted off the ground by a *mistral*, the high velocity wind there. Within a day, we both had terrible colds and decided to head west to the area near Toulouse and Bordeaux. We knew there would be less sunshine, but at least the winds would not be so strong.

We looked in the local newspapers and found listings for twelve abandoned farms. Thây particularly liked one twenty-acre farm surrounded by beautiful, rocky slopes and a green forest. The land, near Thenac, in the Dordogne region, was only one franc (20¢) per square meter, including the three 200-year-old stone buildings that had been used for cattle, pigs, and sheep. Thây really enjoyed walking through the forest there; it was easy for him to envision a walking meditation path. But while we were deliberating, a hailstorm destroyed the owner's vineyard (and thereby his income for the year), and the price of the property rose fourfold. After visiting the other eleven farms, that was still the one Thây liked best, so we decided to buy it even at the higher price.

Our old friend, Le Nguyen Thieu, the last General Secretary of the School of Youth for Social Service, had just arrived in France, and he expressed an interest in joining with us. But the property near Thenac was not arable, and Brother Le knew that he and his family would need to farm to support themselves. So we located a fifty-acre farm with five old stone buildings just three kilometers away, and Le Nguyen Thieu, on our behalf, bought both farms and moved there with his family and a half dozen other recently arrived refugees. We named the properties "Upper Hamlet" (the Thenac property) and "Lower Hamlet" (the farm in Loubès-Bernac), and we called both hamlets together "Làng Hông," literally "Persimmon Village." It was named after the retreat center we had planned to build in Vietnam that was never realized.

In 1973, a beautiful parcel of land in the forested highlands of Vietnam was acquired for us in the hopes that we could return to Vietnam and start a retreat center for social workers. This land had been chosen by Thây Chau Toan, the second director of SYSS. Chau Toan was an artist and the best flower arranger I have ever known. He was a dear younger brother in the Dharma who loved, cherished, and cared for Thây Nhat Hanh.

In 1973, Thây Chau Toan wrote to us describing the beautiful parcel of land he had found. There were tall trees, huge boulders, and a lovely, winding creek. His plans for the center were like a flower arrangement: "There are three giant oaks near the creek, where we can sit for tea meditation. There is a wonderful corner with sim flowers and small pine trees where we can hang hammocks and make a playground for children. And there is much fertile land near the creek, where we can build houses for families." We wanted to plant persimmon trees and sell the fruit to support the center, so we named this retreat center Làng Hông, "Persimmon Village." But Thây Chau Toan never realized his wonderful "flower arrangement." He died of a heart attack in June 1974.

In southwestern France, where we found these two parcels of land, the varieties of plums that are grown for drying are among the most delicious in the world, so we decided to "translate" Làng Hông into French as "Village des Pruniers" and into English as "Plum Village." In the Lower Hamlet, adults and children planted 1,250 plum

Plum Village Plums

Prized as the preeminent plum of Europe, the Prune of Agen has a sweetness reaching well above fifty percent of the register of fruit sugars found in cured fruit. This truly distinctive fruit of the Aquitainian lowland regions of southwestern France is renowned for three unique qualities: the highly aromatic flavor of the cured fruit, the dense, fine texture of the yellow flesh of this dark-skinned plum, and the small, thin, smooth quality of the pit, which separates easily from the fruit when the fruit is eaten fresh or processed.

The Prune d'Agen has evolved over time through the steady, creative labor of the early French growers of the Agen region. The character of this tree reveals and transforms the landscape where it is grown. For centuries this important plant has been cultivated with love and attention, with the good water of the Agen region and with the deep, ancient soil of southwestern France as its source.

—Wendy Johnson

Ode to a Plum Village Plum

When I arrived at Plum Village
you clung tenaciously to the tree
Small, hard, and green.

Today, your hesitant blush
Hints at the future
ripe, succulent, sweet.

Today, your taste
sour and astringent
would pucker my mouth.

Before I leave
My teeth will puncture your
dark purple skin.
I will bite deeply into your
soft yielding flesh.

And I will lick your sticky juices
from the corners of my
mouth.

—Mary Thompson

Panorama of Lower Hamlet on the left and a glimpse of the Upper Hamlet on the right

trees, including 750 that were purchased from donations by children who knew that the money raised from the sale of the plums would go to hungry children in Vietnam and other Third World countries. It has been a lot of work caring for these trees, but by 1990, they already began to bear fruit, and the 1992 harvest was six tons!

In October 1982, we left Sweet Potato and moved to Plum Village. At first there were only Thây, myself, Brother Le, his family, and the other recently arrived refugees. That first year, we discovered how extraordinary Plum Village is. In February, when the oak, linden, and poplar trees were still bare, millions of green buds sprang out from the cold, rocky soil in the forest of the Upper Hamlet, and in early March, fragile, yellow buds and petals of thousands and thousands of daffodils opened their delicate wings and waved at us. Because of their enchanting beauty, Thây named that hillside Dharmakaya Store, "the store of the Dharma body." We don't know why, but the other farms in the area do not have such

hidden treasures of daffodils. Thây proposed that we organize a Daffodil Festival to welcome these little angel bodhisattvas. Each year, people from Bordeaux, Toulouse, and other nearby cities come and spend the first Sunday in March with us walking in the sea of yellow daffodils, listening to a Dharma talk by Thây, and enjoying tea meditation, songs, and dancing by the children. What a gift from Heaven and Earth!

We wanted to open Plum Village to social workers and others needing a retreat, so as soon as we moved there, we began clearing out the old buildings, putting in wooden floors, and making simple beds. In the summer of 1982, we received 100 people; in 1983, 200 people; and since 1991, more than 1,000 people have come each summer from all over the world. During the July 15 to August 15 Summer Opening, people register in advance to stay at least one week, sharing the practice of mindfulness with us under the guidance of Thây Nhat Hanh and his Sangha. Together, we practice sitting meditation, walking meditation, tea meditation, work meditation, and Dharma discussion. It is not an intensive course. Families and friends practice joyfully together,

and every day Thây gives a talk in Vietnamese, English, or French, with simultaneous translation into those and other languages. We offer many cultural activities for Vietnamese children—the older children teach the younger ones about their homeland, and there is a lot of singing. We also have beautiful programs for Western children. Every week, we organize a festival, such as Welcoming the Full Moon, Happy Continuation of Our Ancestors, Staying in Touch with the Suffering of the Boat People and the Victims of the Atomic Bombs, and Thanksgiving.

The teachings of Thây Nhat Hanh during the summer retreat are for children and adults to create peace in themselves and in the world. The unique aspect of Plum Village as a retreat center is the focus on children. We don't force them, but the children are invited to join us for the short periods of sitting meditation, walking meditation, tea meditation (the children have "lemonade meditation"), and eating meals quietly, with awareness and appreciation. It turns out that many children practice mindfulness better than their parents, and when they return home, they remind their parents to come back to the present

moment and enjoy the many wonders that are all around them. The Summer Retreat is one of the great joys of Plum Village.

After four years of farming in the French way, Brother Le Nguyen Thieu and the other refugees realized that they could not earn enough to support themselves and their families, and in 1987, they moved out. At about the same time, a number of Vietnamese monks, nuns, and laypersons, and several Westerners asked if they could stay year-round to study Buddhism and practice mindfulness with Thây. As a result, a residential practice community of about fifty members has formed. Due to the lack of year-round facilities, we can only accept this number of trainees. More than half are monks and nuns. Thây has developed a four-year Dharma teacher training program to produce "agents of transformation" for Vietnam and the West. Trainees first learn to transform their own "internal knots" and become "solid as a mountain and fresh as a flower," so they can share the Dharma through their own insight and their own "being," not just from books. But we also study books.

Little Bamboo playing violin among the treasure house of yellow daffodils

Annabel Laity, Sister True Virtue, is an Englishwoman, well-suited for the responsibility of teaching the Dharma and also helping with the administrative work of Plum Village. Thanks to her, we have been able to accept new trainees as well as negotiate with the French authorities and keep up with the administrative work. We now grow much of our food organically, including vegetables that are difficult to find outside of Vietnam. At times the slugs eat half our crop, but we do not discriminate. We know they need to live too! Every evening in Spring, practitioners go to the greenhouse with their flashlights and pick the slugs off the leaves, put them in a large container, and carry them to the forest, where they can eat the tender leaves there.

Every year, in early April, plum blossoms light up the Lower Hamlet. Looking at the orchard, we feel as though we are looking at the night sky, with millions of tiny stars. Mornings in Plum Village in spring, fall, and winter are usually foggy, and we often have the impression during walking meditation that we are walking among the clouds. Sunsets and full moons are also wonderful occasions for us to practice walking meditation, and they provide inspiration for many to discover their artistic talents. Many Plum Village residents have discovered hidden musical and artistic talents just by living in such a joyful community.

At the request of Western friends, Thây sometimes leads a special retreat in English during the month of June. The transformation for many Western friends who cannot stay year-round has been great. I have seen people who, after just three weeks of strong practice—listening to the teachings and living in the community—have become fresh as flowers. We all need a place we can go to refresh ourselves. I realized this when we were working at the School of Youth for Social Service and I see it today. Plum Village is a joyful, international community, the fruit of many experiences, and we continue to learn and practice.

Transformation and Peace

"Those who practice mindful living will inevitably transform themselves
and their way of life. They will live more simply and have
more time to enjoy themselves, their friends, and their natural environment,
and to offer joy to others and alleviate others' suffering."

—Thich Nhat Hanh

Our True Heritage

Thich Nhat Hanh

The cosmos is filled with precious gems.
I want to offer a handful of them to you this morning.
Each moment you are alive is a gem,
shining through and containing Earth and sky,
water and clouds.

It needs you to breathe gently
for the miracles to be displayed.
Suddenly you hear the birds singing,
the pines chanting,
see the flowers blooming,
the blue sky,
the white clouds,
the smile and the marvelous look
of your beloved.

You, the richest person on Earth,
who have been going around begging,
stop being the destitute child.
Come back and claim your heritage.
Enjoy your happiness
and offer it to everyone.
Cherish this very moment.
Let go of the stream of distress
and embrace life fully in your arms.

Finding Our True Home

Jina van Hengel

When a tree is planted in the earth, it is connected to the earth by its roots. The whole of the tree is nourished and supported by the earth, and the earth is nourished and supported by the tree. Roots are the place where interactions and transformations take place. They are the energy that flows out of the trunk and into the earth, as well as into the sky, interacting with the sun, the clouds, and everything in the cosmos. When we cut ourselves off

Sister Jina and Ellen: "A lotus for you, a Buddha-to-be."

from something, we suppress the flow of energy, and this blocked energy builds up inside of us and makes us restless. When we are cut off from our culture, we don't feel at home anywhere, and we have the desire to be rooted.

We may try to find a new tradition to root ourselves in, accepting what we like about our new "home" and regarding as irrelevant what we do not like: "This doesn't really pertain to me." This is another form of rejection, and it means that not all of the rooting energy is flowing freely. Although we call it our new home, we do not really feel "at home," and sooner or later, this blocked energy will need to be released. Only when our rooting energy is flowing freely can we find a resting place, a true home.

Rooting energy and the means to release all the obstacles that block its path are available right now. Many practices are offered to help us allow this energy to flow freely, such as conscious breathing and smiling, walking meditation, the Beginning Anew Ceremony, the Peace Treaty, and others. Through such practices as these, we take root in each other and everything around us. We grow together as a brother, a sister, or a family. Connected with everything, we feel "at home" wherever we are. There is a place of rest right inside us. When we find our true home, we are a healthy tree, with interactions and transformations taking place throughout our root system. We are firmly planted in our home, like a tree firmly planted in earth and sky.

One time the Buddha was shot by Mara with poisonous arrows, but as soon as the arrows touched him, they turned into flowers. Thây advises us to practice diligently so that we can create a body like the Buddha's. I did not understand what kind of body that was, so I decided to meditate on this story. I followed my breathing and imagined having a strong body that did not allow any arrows to enter. Sitting with stability, I saw that, indeed, the arrows did not enter my

---

❋ The Lotus Rap

Well it's Cool Kid Sid* around the block,
you know, the one who dances to rap and rock.
He was born as a prince in southern Nepal.
His parents thought he was the greatest of all.
A fortune teller told them to raise Sid with care,
or else he'd leave home and they'd all despair.
He grew up with everything a kid could want.
But with all that, he was still nonchalant.
He was a sports jock
and a straight A student,
never lost his cool,
and was always prudent.
Even though he grew up in the lap of luxury,
he was still not truly ha-ha-happy.
One day he went outside of the wall
and his high hopes
started to fall.
He saw suffering
and much, much more—
there was an old man, a sick man,
and a dead man on the floor.
Then there was a monk walking down the street.
Sid said, "Yo man, you're looking pretty neat."
He was talking in the most awesome way.
He was teaching peace all through the day.
That was where it all began.
From then on Sid was a Buddha-man.

—Ty Eppsteiner

*Siddhartha

Eveline offers a flower arrangement for Thây's Dharma talk

body. But I also saw heaps of broken and bent arrows around me. This was quite different from the Buddha being surrounded by flowers. I looked more deeply and saw that the Buddha's body is a body of insight. It does not receive the arrows because as soon as they touch it, they are transformed into flowers. The insight body recognizes the true nature of the arrows, sees what they are made of, and thus transforms them immediately. Arrows cannot enter such a body because they no longer exist.

To develop or strengthen our insight body, we practice mindful living. When this body becomes strong, our rooting energy flows freely. We stand like a tree with our roots dug down into the earth and our branches stretched out connecting and interacting with all that is, and we see clearly what needs to be transformed for the benefit of all. Happy rooting!

Finding Peace after a Lifetime of War

Claude Thomas

I was trained to be a soldier from the day I was born, by the way I was brought up and the things I was encouraged to do—hunt, kill, dominate, rule, and control my environment. I was taught not to be mindful, not to be thoughtful.

My father was a schoolteacher. My mother never graduated from school. The environment in my house was not different from most of the houses around me. It was filled with anger and violence, which I did not understand because I did not have the skills to understand.

I went into the military, and then to Vietnam at the age of seventeen. I did not know what else to do, and my father suggested it would make a man out of me. I was a high school athlete, so I was already used to discipline and exerting physical strength. A local journalist said that if he had to charge a hill with anyone, he would want it to be me.

On my second day in the military, I realized it was not a good choice. But I did not know I could get out. So I did the next best thing: I learned to be the best soldier I could. I trained to be a ranger, which meant that I became very skilled in killing. The military is only about killing. It is not about defense. It is about offense.

In my training, I learned to dehumanize the enemy, and in the process, I became dehumanized. I remember a huge drill sergeant standing in my face screaming obscenities, taking out his penis and urinating on me. There was nothing I

could do because I did not know I could do anything. And I was unaware at the time how deeply those kinds of actions affect human beings. Experiences like that never go away.

My job in Vietnam was to crew helicopter gunships. Before my eighteenth birthday I had been

Thuc Hiên in front of the Lower Hamlet bamboo grove

responsible for the deaths of hundreds of people. This was not my first experience of war. There was the war before the war, and the war after the war, and the war that continues to rage on a daily basis all over the world. My life in high school was one form of war; my family was another form of war. I was prepared to kill before I killed, because I was so filled with anger, resentment, hurt, despair, and suffering. And my story is not unusual. There are similar stories every day all over the world. There will never be peace on Earth until we have peace within ourselves. We have to be able to look deeply into the nature of our suffering—to touch, embrace and hold it—before we can touch peace.

In 1967, when I was shot down for the fifth time, the pilot and the aircraft commander were killed and the gunner was critically wounded. As I lay pinned in the overturned helicopter, I could smell the fuel leaking and I could hear the gunfire hitting the helicopter. I was convinced I would die and believed that I *should* die. I did not want to survive because I hated myself and what I had done. But I did not die. I was hospitalized for nine months, and at the age of twenty I was discharged from the military.

The Plum Village Bell Tower, designed in the traditional way

On my way home, as I walked across the airport in Newark to change planes—a highly decorated soldier in uniform—I was approached by a very attractive young woman. I thought she was interested in me or wanted to talk, but when she got within inches of my face, she spit on me. I went to a bar and got drunk, and I stayed drunk and high for the next fifteen years. I needed intoxicants because I had no skills or ability to touch the depth of suffering in my life. By not being able to embrace my suffering, I could not transform it, and it leaked out in indirect ways. My life was full of anger, rage, and violence; it was the only way I knew to be.

I joined in the antiwar movement, not because I believed in peace, but because I believed that if you are going to fight a war, you might as well fight it to win. My thinking has since changed radically: I'm convinced that we *do not need* to fight. It is an insane proposition that because we are human beings it is natural for us to fight and kill. Through mindfulness there are ways to resolve conflicts without violence. I experienced the peace movement as simply another war movement. It was violent and ugly, and Vietnam veterans were a prized possession as long as we could serve their purpose. But when it came to healing, they, like the rest of the country, were not there to help us.

Beginning in 1970, I began to leave the United States on a regular basis. I was embarrassed to be an American, and besides I could not stand to turn on the TV anymore and listen to the talk about the war. In 1974 I bought a one-way ticket from London to Tehran. I did not speak the language, I did not have any idea what went on in Iran, I just knew that it was far away. I thought the insanity of my life rested outside of me. I felt that if I could find the right place or the right teacher, it would heal me. What I was seeking was outside of myself, because I did not have the skills or the encouragement to look inward.

In Iran, it became more and more difficult to keep the lid on the untouched issues of war and violence in my life. I was living in a country where the secret police (the Savak) would come into a family and take away every male person above the age of sixteen and imprison them without a trial for ten years, and I saw this happen often. I reacted to these conditions in the only way I knew, in anger and violence. One taxicab driver stiffed me for fifteen cents, and I totaled his taxi with my bare hands. I continued to put myself at risk, hoping that I would die, because I could not stand to live with what was going on inside me.

One night the police took me away and interrogated me for ten days, trying to get me to sign a paper that I was a spy. During the interrogation, they broke four ribs on one side, five ribs on the other, cracked both my cheekbones, ruptured my spleen, sodomized me, and then just threw me out on the street. I survived, although I did not want to. My response was to act out more violently, and I ended up in jail two more times. I had no other recourse than to act out the anger, to act out in kind, to punish the punisher. I did not know any other way.

I have no idea how or when it began to turn around for me. In 1990, I shut myself in my house, afraid to leave, no longer able to touch society because of all that it represented for me. When I walked outside and heard jets flying overhead, I cringed because I could see treelines going up in napalm and young Vietnamese running from villages. When I walked into the grocery store, I could not take a can of vegetables off the shelf because I was afraid it was booby-trapped. The feelings were vivid, but this time I did not run away. I knew that in order for it to be transformed, I had to stay with my reality.

I heard about Thich Nhat Hanh from a social worker in Cambridge, Massachusetts, who told me about a Zen monk who had had some success helping Vietnam veterans to heal. She did not say that he was Vietnamese. Six months later, someone else told me about a retreat for Vietnam veterans run by this same man. I telephoned the retreat center, not because I wanted to, but because nothing in my life was working and I did not know what else to do. I wanted my life to be different. So, terrified, I went to the retreat.

Part of my military training was to operate in small units of four or five people. We were dropped in to gather information, assassinate, or destroy. If during an operation any of us became wounded and could not continue, our job was to kill them because they would slow us down. I knew how to build walls against terror. I have come in on a helicopter looking at the fifty caliber tracer rounds come at me, glowing as big as softballs, knowing that when you see one, there are five that you do not. I learned ways to deny terror and to just go forward. That is what got me to the retreat. But when this Vietnamese monk walked into the room, sat down, and I

looked into his face, I started to cry. I realized in the moment of him sitting there that I did not know the Vietnamese people in any other way than as the enemy. They were the enemy, and if they were the enemy then I did not know how to relate to anyone else in the world other than as the enemy. Everyone was the enemy.

the tears I shed yesterday have become rain
nh

One of the first things this monk said was, "You veterans are the light at the tip of the candle. You burn hot. You have the ability through your experience to help in the transformation of the world, to transform the violence, to transform the hate, to transform the despair. You need to talk." And he said, "The non-veterans need to listen. The veterans deserve to be understood. To understand someone, you need to place yourself in his skin."

All my life when I tried to talk about these things, people always went away. They said, "You're too intense. I can't deal with you. I've got to leave." I have come to understand that what they were really saying is, "In relationship with you, I am touching parts of myself that I do not want to touch."

Thich Nhat Hanh said that the non-veterans were more responsible for the war than the veterans, and I knew the truth in that. He was articulating things I had known all my life. Since the end of the war, more than 58,000 Vietnam vets, young men and women, have killed themselves.

In the war, 57,693 Americans died in combat. I can be sure that there are one or two veterans in every group of homeless people I see on the street, and many have ended up in prisons. We have been marginalized.

I did not know what to do. I approached Sister Chân Không after the retreat. I wanted to make amends for the killing, but I did not have the courage to say that. All I said was, "I would really like to go back to Vietnam." And she smiled, "You need to come to Plum Village first. Let us help you." I said, "I cannot afford to come." She said, "We will buy your ticket." This was my enemy. No one in this country had ever offered me an opportunity like that to heal.

In the summers in Plum Village, most of the Vietnamese people live in the Lower Hamlet. When I arrived, Sister Chân Không told me that I would live in the Lower Hamlet. So there I was in a community of 400 Vietnamese, and every place I turned, another terrifying memory would come up from the war. I could not work hard enough, I could not keep busy enough to get away from those memories. When I wanted to talk to somebody, I would approach a monk or a nun and try to explain what was going on, saying, "I see the young Vietnamese women in their *ao-dai* coming into the zendo, and I remember a gun run in a village where I was responsible for killing thirty or forty people." When I would start to talk like that, the monks and nuns would say, "The past is in the past. There is only the present moment, and it is beautiful."

I did not know how to deal with that. So I did not say anything until one day I began to talk about the war and when I got the same spiel from a monk, I turned around in real anger and said, "The past is not in the past for me. It is in the present moment and it is ugly." I talked to Sister Chân Không about this, and she said, "If you are living intensely in the present moment, the past and the future are also there. You just need to be with them like still water." That was all I needed.

I went back to Plum Village the following year, and have since returned twice, each visit I have to confront myself over and over again. I was victimized, but I cannot continue to maintain the posture of being a victim. I need to heal. I need to transform. I need to challenge the ideas that I have been subjected to throughout my life.

Thich Nhat Hanh always teaches the Five Precepts. The first is: "Aware of the suffering caused by the destruction of life, I vow to cultivate compassion and to learn the ways of protecting the lives of people, animals, plants, and minerals. I am determined not to kill, not to let others kill, and not to condone any act of killing in my thinking and way of life." For me, this is a lifelong practice, and it begins with getting in close touch with the feelings in me and working moment by moment to embrace them and to transform them into love and understanding.

Vets' Retreat

Anne Cushman

As the daughter of an Army general who served three tours in Vietnam, I went to Thich Nhat Hanh's retreat for Veterans seeking to understand and help heal my own family's past. Like hundreds of thousands of children, my childhood was shaped by my father's participation in the Vietnam War: his repeated, prolonged absences and the never-acknowledged terror that he would not come back alive drove my mother to an emotional breakdown and left deep wounds in my heart.

At the retreat, I had the opportunity not only to contact and heal my own hurt, but to be touched and inspired by the practice of those who had experienced the suffering of war far more painfully and directly than I had. About half of the eighty-five participants were veterans, seeking healing for bodies, minds, and spirits battered by combat.

"You are the light at the tip of the candle," Thây told the veterans. "You know what the reality of war is, and you can show it to us." Throughout the retreat, the veterans' courage, honesty, and insights were truly a candle flame illuminating the path for all of us. While nurturing the seeds of mindfulness and peace through quiet breathing, smiling, sitting, and walking, we also began to examine the nature of aggression.

Thây asked us to look deeply into the roots of war in our society, our families, and our own hearts—the seeds of violence, fear, and hatred that can be found everywhere, even within the antiwar movement. War, he told us, is not just waged by soldiers: all of us participate in it, and all of us must help heal the damage. The veterans are "the hand that grasped the fire," he said, but the order to do so came from the whole body, and the whole body suffers as a result. As part of the body of society, all of us are co-responsible for our country's actions, he said. If we do not understand our co-responsibility, our nation will do the same thing again and again.

At the end of the retreat, Thây led us in hugging meditation, telling the veterans, "If you hug one Vietnamese person, you hug us all." Afterwards, we did walking meditation in the dark to a lake, several veterans carrying a paper decorated with the names of those who had died in the Vietnam war. Standing under the stars holding candles, we sang the "Two Promises" while we burned the paper and scattered the ashes into the shimmering water: "I vow to develop understanding in order to live peaceably with people, animals, and plants. I vow to develop my compassion, in order to protect the lives of people, animals, and plants."

I left the retreat inspired by the power of mindfulness practice to heal even the deepest of wounds. Practicing with the veterans was a great opportunity to support them in their healing process while going further into my own. As Thây said early in the retreat, "If the non-veterans practice in order to have insight, the veterans will be healed. And if the veterans practice in order to have insight, the non-veterans will be healed. Because we inter-are."

Staggering Meditation

Alan Cutter

In November 1992, Arnie Kotler, Therese Fitzgerald, and Claude Thomas came to share a Day of Mindfulness with a group of Vietnam veteran ministers. We all could sit, but walking meditation was difficult for a few of us. One man lost his legs in Vietnam; I injured a hip and knee during an incident and cannot walk slowly and deliberately without a cane. I mentioned to Therese that during the walking meditation, as I sat on the porch and watched, I had felt left out and separated from the group; half in jest, I said that what I needed was some form of "staggering meditation." She replied, "It's up to you to invent it."

That day I had left my wooden cane in a corner of my room at the retreat center. For years I have kept it hidden, having learned how to compensate for and disguise my painful problem with walking. That "stick" was a reminder of things I wanted to forget. I did not want to remember "Cripple Corner" in Danang, an intersection near a Vietnamese hospital where maimed Vietnamese soldiers, surrounded by canes, crutches, and makeshift wheelchairs, would gather to wait for an American convoy of large trucks to pass, hoping to be able to throw themselves, or be thrown by friends, under the huge tires so that their families could collect some monetary compensation from the U.S. government. Yet I could not forget, a few years ago, watching a parade in Wheeling, West Virginia. I knelt down beside my young son, and my hip went out and I could not get up, and I was one with the soldiers of years before, a "cripple" by the roadside. Shame, disgust, and despair welled up within me; my helplessness found a focus on that hated cane, and in my anger I would not use it.

When I returned to my room later that afternoon, I sat and thought about inventing "staggering meditation." I decided that I would go for a walk, and rather than take my "stick" along as a necessary evil and out of anxiety over falling, I would "invite" my cane to be my helper. "Please come and be my companion," I said. So we set out to walk into the nearby city center. As we made our way along the sidewalks, I tried being aware not only of my breath but of my feet and of the wooden cane in my hand. Many emotions and thoughts came and I greeted both the pleasant ones and the not-so-pleasant ones and invited them to join us in our walk. After a while, I became less aware of these emotions and thoughts and more aware of the ground on which I was walking, the beauty and gentle warmth of the evening, and the people around me. I even became thankful for the companion which supported me.

As I have continued my "staggering meditation" with my companion, I have tried to think deeply about this practice. For so many years, because of my anger, I deprived myself of support that I needed to be fully mobile. When I did seek that support, I was motivated more by a fear of falling than anything else. I have come to an awareness that my companion is a gift that helps connect me not only with the ground, but also with the many others who for a variety of reasons cannot walk easily, but who also stagger. When I am connected with these brothers and sisters, I no longer feel separated or left out. Rather than a reminder of a terrible past, I have uncovered a deep root of present meaning in this "tree" that I hug in my hand.

LA MARCHE

Joyeux

Texte et Musique: Jean-Pierre Maradan

Watering the Seed of Mindfulness

Peter Matthiessen

In late March of 1991, on the way to a retreat for environmentalists to be led by the eminent Vietnamese Zen master, poet, and peace activist Thich Nhat Hanh, I took time for a walk up Malibu Creek, in the Malibu Canyon State Park. Spring songbirds were numerous, and a golden eagle sailed high overhead, crossing the Santa Catalina Mountains of the Coast Range, and from a bridge over the creek I saw a heavy brown-furred animal half-hidden behind rocks close to the bank. From its striped ears, I knew it was a bobcat, stalking three coot that had come ashore into the sedges. So intent was it upon its prey that, moving out into the open, it looked back just once, the sun catching the oval of light fur around the lynxish eyes. However, the coot, sensing danger, swam away from shore, and as the bobcat made its way downstream, striped bobbed tail twitching in frustration, the slate gray birds with their ivory bills followed along, just off the bank, peering and craning to see where the wildcat had got to.

The bobcat or bay lynx is not uncommon, but it is elusive, difficult to see; I have crossed paths with it perhaps eight times in fifty years of wildlife observation, usually as it crossed a trail or a night road. This was the first one I had ever watched for minutes at a time—ten minutes at the least—in open sunlight of mid-afternoon, scarcely fifty feet away, a stirring event that seemed to me an auspicious sign for the environmentalists' retreat that would begin that evening.

Originally the retreat was to take place at Ojai, but in recent weeks, due to housing complications, it had been shifted to Camp Sholom, a

Thây in the Bamboo Grove, Lower Hamlet

Jewish retreat in the Santa Catalinas, perhaps five miles inland from the coast; the camp lies in a hollow in the dry chaparral hills, in a grove of sycamore and live oak where two brooks come together. The hills were green and the brooks rushing from the heavy rains, which muddied the ground beneath the huge white tent and moved the whole retreat indoors.

My host was James Soshin Thornton, a student of Maezumi Roshi and the founding lawyer of the Los Angeles office of the Natural Resources Defense Council, which together with the Nathan

Cummings Foundation, the Ojai Foundation, and the Community of Mindful Living, had sponsored the retreat. One of my own Zen students, Dennis Snyder, was also present, and so were several environmental acquaintances and friends-of-friends.

Zazen, which took place in the meeting hall on the first evening, after some welcoming remarks by Thich Nhat Hanh, Joan Halifax of Ojai, and James Thornton, was a new experience for most of the environmentalists among the 225 retreatants, some of whom were later obliged to move to chairs, but they persevered bravely and by the week's end, were sitting as assiduously as all the rest.

"When you take care of the environmentalist," said Thich Nhat Hanh, urging the use of a gentle smile to help us pay attention to each moment, "you take care of the environment." This remark might have been the theme of the whole retreat.

Thich Nhat Hanh, called "Thây" by his students, is a small, large-toothed man with a broad smile and kind, smiling eyes, so youthful in appearance that one scarcely believes he was nominated in 1968 (by Martin Luther King) for the Nobel Peace Prize.

In his first Dharma talk next morning (on breathing meditation: "When I breathe in, I am aware of my eyes...of the lovely morning...of my heart....") he stood in brown robes in the early sun that shimmered from the small hard shiny leaves of live oak and poured through the windowed wall behind him, filtered by a lovely wooden screen of six carved panels that Joan Halifax believes came originally from China. Like chinks of sun through the brown rosettes of the screen, Thây's white teeth glinted in that childlike wide-eyed smile.

"Sometimes we believe we would like to be someone else, but of course we cannot be someone else, we can only be ourselves, and even that is very difficult....To be ourselves, we must be in the present moment, and to be in the present moment we must follow our breath, be one with our breath, for otherwise we are overtaken by emotions and events...."

Thây's daily talks were pointed up by intermittent bell notes rung by his attendant Therese Fitzgerald (formerly of San Francisco Zen Center), and all meals, eaten in silence, were also punctuated by a bell, to remind retreatants to pay attention to this present moment.

Insight depends upon awareness of this moment, according to Thây's teaching, which leads inevitably to compassion and a natural state of being. His teaching returns again and again to the soft image of a flower, "showing its heart" as it opens to the sun. The *mudra* of *gassho* he likens to a closed lotus, the hands opening outward in gratitude and thanks for this extraordinary existence, in the way that a bean sprout opens, smiling, to the sun and wind. That half-smile on the lips will lead to an unforced well-being, contributing to a sincere joy in one's practice. "If your practice is not pleasurable," then some other practice might be more suitable, says Thây.

On the first evening, an informal panel—Thây's associate, the Vietnamese nun Sister Chân

Sister Chân Không

Không, James Thornton, and Randy Hayes of the Rainforest Action Network, also Joan Halifax and myself—took questions from the gathering of perhaps 225 persons that filled the meeting hall right to the walls. Sister Chân Không, a small dynamic person who administers one hundred social workers in Vietnam (all unknown to one another, since they may be harassed by the government), was articulate and eloquent; like Thich Nhat Hanh, she counseled returning to the breath as the foundation of this moment, of our very being. And the panel agreed that in time of distress, we must go into that distress, deeper and deeper, become one with it.

On other occasions, in a sweet voice, Sister Chân Không burst into song, manifesting the joy in this moment that Thây talks about. Discussing the anger she sometimes feels, seeing the waste of water and materials in our bathrooms and kitchens, she says she cures this by singing aloud, "When I go to the bathroom (kitchen, etc.), I feel happy, because I have learned to breathe deeply...." (After Thây's Dharma talk on the precepts, she remarked, "When you are truly mindful, you don't need the precepts.")

Each day began with two early periods of strong zazen, followed by recitation from the sutras or, on one occasion, a fine letter to Thây from an environmental lawyer in the group who stressed the need for the spiritual base for environmental work that has been sadly lacking in most organizations. After silent breakfast in the dining hall, down along the creek, Thây would talk to us again, in a Dharma talk that one day ran close to two hours.

"We are only real when we are one with our breathing—our walking, our eating—and it is then that everything around us becomes real....Eating a bean, be conscious of the true nature of that bean, the structure, all the non-bean elements that make up that bean, and permit it to exist. If you look into a flower penetratingly, you will see the sun, the minerals, the water that make up the flower, which contains all the non-flower elements in the world, just as a Buddhist contains all the non-Buddhist elements."

Thây offers documentary film crew a cup of tea

Thây's eyes sometimes remain sad even when he is smiling, and more than once during the week he expressed distress over the actions of President Bush in the Gulf War, which had almost deterred him from making his annual visit to this country. He spoke to us of "sowing the seed of peace in our land," and attending to "the President Bush within ourselves . . ." as we might attend to our greed, ignorance, and anger.

"Take tender care of your anger, with mindfulness...don't suppress it...it is you. You have been watering the seed of your anger rather than the seed of your mindfulness; the anger comes from lack of understanding, and it comes very easily....If mindfulness is there, you are protected from anger and from fear."

And he spoke to us strongly against "sowing the seed of suffering" in our speech and actions.

Another day, he pointed out our compulsive behavior, our inability to stop: the more we eat (sleep, telephone, watch television, drive in our car)—the more we fill the emptiness, in short—the hungrier we become. We must fill every moment, we cannot just be. "How can we stop the arms race when we cannot stop ourselves?"

Following the Dharma talk came walking meditation in the hills, then lunch, then afternoon meetings with various leaders, late afternoon zazen, supper, and more evening meetings, followed by a last period of formal zazen. All of these events except zazen were interspersed with semi-spiritual musical presentations by two guitarist-singers, an evening of entertainment, and even a Passover supper, or *seder*. At times, Thây appeared vaguely mystified by these secular events, which were not, however, permitted to alter the warm and yet serious tone of the retreat.

Despite his gentle manner, Thich Nhat Hanh is a strict teacher with a strong adherence to the precepts. Talking informally one evening over green tea in his room, we discussed the fact that many if not most Zen teachers transgress the precepts in one way or another, and he said wryly, "They have the idea that this is all right for enlightened people."

He went on to describe his Rinzai training in Vietnam, where he became a monk in 1942 and founded the Tiep Hien Order in 1964; I had not realized that Rinzai Zen, which traveled eastward from China to Korea and Japan, then the United States, had also made its way south into Southeast Asia, where Theravadin Buddhism had held sway for centuries.

As the days passed and the rain ceased and concentration deepened, Thich Nhat Hanh's mild tones came and went like some wonderful soft voice from faraway in the mysterious stacks of a huge library. At times the whole brown-robed being seemed to shine, as if he and the sun-filled screen, the mountain light, were now all one. "We have to be a little bit mindful just to notice the moon, but we don't appreciate the intensity, the beauty of our life, until we are truly mindful in each moment."

❄

Keeping Plum Village in Mind

When I first came to Plum Village, I was recovering from cancer. The physical spaces of both hamlets comforted me, especially the meditation halls with their 200-year-old stone buildings and smooth new wooden floors. Those rooms, Thây's teachings, and the practice of breathing the fresh country air restored my heart.

Back at home that fall, I felt some desperate moments. My energy seemed inadequate, but a vision protected me and new habits helped. Where once I had raced to get through traffic lights before they turned red, I now welcomed the opportunity to stop and remember Plum Village. Just thinking of Plum Village calmed me down.

—Robert Schaibly

❄

Learning True Love

I often wonder how Sister Chân Không was able to survive all the pain and suffering she witnessed in Vietnam. I ponder Thây's poems and wonder how his heart has been able to bear such pain. I am deeply grateful to both of them and all their associates who work so steadily to plant seeds of compassion in this world. My husband and I feel overwhelmed by the violence in our city. At times, I long to be in a place where I don't hear gunshots every evening. Then I read more of Sister Chân Không's memoirs, Learning True Love, *and feel inspired. I know she is with me and that I have a large Sangha that supports me as I make my way. I am deeply grateful for the existence of this wonderful web throughout the world, and I am thankful for Thây's teaching and the precepts that so clearly bring us back to the present moment.*

—Kathleen Biswas

Spiritual Footing for Environmentalists

Grove Burnett

I have been practicing environmental law for twenty years, representing public interest environmental organizations in five states in the Western United States, both national and grassroots, on a wide variety of issues ranging from pollution of our air and water, cutting of our ancient forests, and protection of our vanishing wildlife. Being a lawyer has offered me a strangely unique perspective that no other work in the environmental movement—or for that matter our society—can provide. Sadly, the legal profession is a pretty unwholesome gathering that practices all too diligently the universal principles of greed, hatred, and delusion! It's a challenge that continuously tests my practice.

I came to this ancient Buddhist practice of mindfulness by way of the occupational hazard of this movement and all activists: burnout. I crashed, suffering a severe physical illness and a classic life crisis. In the darkest hour of all this, however, some door opened and I stumbled into a seven-day Vipassana retreat with Jack Kornfield. Suddenly and with a clarity that changed my life, I understood what I was looking for: that hole inside of me that I had been trying to fill with all sorts of things during my life could only be filled by a genuine spiritual teaching and practice. I've been studying and practicing in the Vipassana tradition with Jack for the last five years, and have attended several retreats with Thây Nhat Hanh, where my wife, Linda, and I received the precepts.

The most compelling issue facing the environmental movement—at least the mainstream movement in the U.S.—is its lack of spiritual footing. Without a solid spiritual foundation, the movement lacks wholeness and wisdom and the personal happiness and effectiveness of those involved is severely compromised. The environmental movement struggles desperately to ground itself on something other than standard political and social rhetoric; without a genuine spiritual grounding, however, it is largely rootless, casting about for a center. We all know and feel that the present environmental destruction is unjust and unacceptable, yet we tilt about trying to fit those feelings into inadequate political frameworks. What we are really searching for is a deeper religious and spiritual framework in which to articulate and act on these feelings.

This lack of solid spiritual footing means that those of us involved in the struggle suffer, on a personal basis. Too often—I see this with all my colleagues all over the country—environmentalists operate from a level of panic and crisis in our mission to rescue the planet. We become warriors battling in a war zone—confronting one impending disaster and crisis after another, trying to save the planet. The results, of course, are predictable: being dedicated soldiers we take no time for our own personal and spiritual nourishment and our lives, health, families, friendships suffer and sometimes break apart under the tension.

In addition, our effectiveness to effect change and relieve suffering is severely compromised as we push ourselves harder, sacrificing our lives for saving the planet, until often we are consuming enormous amounts of time and energy with meager results. The consequence of reduced effectiveness is one that comes with the terrain of being a dedicated, angry activist who has no spiritual place of rest and healing. When we work in the panic zone we begin to think that the best and only strategy is to put other people into the panic zone. Clear thinking and wisdom, of course, are not characteristics of the panic zone and do not produce quality actions or work.

Sister Chân Không on her way to Golden Years Hut

As my personal practice has deepened I have recognized that the mentality of a warrior is not the appropriate model or course for the environmental movement. We don't need warriors—and we certainly don't need more lawyers. What we need are guardians—guardians committed to the middle path of mindfulness and dedicated to the enormous task of restoring and healing our ravaged planet. Guardians who have penetrated the anthropocentric notions of our civilization and who, as Aldo Leopold said, can begin to "think like a mountain" and acknowledge that we are only "plain members of the biotic community."

Grounding our engagement in a spiritual practice offers us the extraordinary opportunity—which has been confirmed in my own life—to find a middle way. Instead of reeling from one crisis to the next, motivated by anger and outrage towards those we deem responsible for the precipitous state of the planet, this practice, with its profoundly spiritual grounding, can bring us to a path of equanimity and peace in what we are doing. This is a profound teaching. We cannot heal our ravaged planet unless we have the ability to heal ourselves. True healing only comes with the surrender of stepping on a spiritual path. Unfortunately, the environmental movement does not have a spiritual path.

Stepping upon the spiritual path, especially the path of mindfulness, has immense rewards for environmentalists and all activists who are committed to active engagement in our society. We environmentalists are frequently overwhelmed by the magnitude of the global environmental crisis and the enormity of the task to restore and heal this fragile planet of ours. Tending to our own healing and spiritual work should be a matter of the highest priority. If environmentalists connect with the profound spiritual dimension of our work, we will be able to acknowledge the need for healing ourselves—not just the planet we are frantically and desperately fighting to preserve.

For myself, the effects of a spiritual practice have been truly rewarding. Not only has my own personal suffering diminished as I have attended to my own healing, but, most surprising to me, my effectiveness as an advocate in the movement has increased dramatically. I did not enter upon this path and take this teaching to become more effective in my work—it was the furthest consideration from my mind. I embarked on this journey to heal my battle-scarred and weary soul and body. The gift of this path, however, has been not only the personal healing—but increased effectiveness in my work.

May all beings be free from suffering.

A Day with Thây at Spirit Rock

Nina Wise

I was still in my nightgown when I heard a knock at the front door. A dark haired woman I didn't recognize stood there, zafu in hand.

"You're Nina?" she asked.

"Yes," I said, perplexed.

"Allan and Marion told me to meet them here. I'm Angelique."

"Oh, come in," I forced myself to be polite, still half asleep, thinking I had fifteen more minutes before having to talk to anyone. "Do you want some tea?"

"Yes," she said, "that would be wonderful."

Angelique sat down while I scurried about, embarrassed by my own irritation at this interruption, making tea, making conversation, gathering my hat, sunglasses, sunscreen, blanket, zafu, water bottle, brushing my teeth, dressing. What should I wear, I wondered, to a gathering of 1,200 people, outdoors from 7 a.m. until 6 p.m., sitting and walking in the unique practice of smiling mindfulness that Thich Nhat Hanh teaches. I pulled out a dress, loose, colorful, and suited for the out-of-doors.

Allan and Marion arrived and the four of us piled into Angelique's car for what we feared would be a massive early morning traffic jam on the road to Spirit Rock. But the way was clear and as we pulled into the newly built road at the center, the dedicated volunteers in orange hats had everything under control. Cars flowed smoothly into designated parking fields and people made their way to a grassy hillside. By the time we arrived, the hill was already populated with hundreds of people. We searched for a spot,

plopped down our pads and pillows, and waited for Thây's arrival. There was an air of eager anticipation as people continued to arrive and find spots higher and higher up the field. I giggled, remembering Wes Nisker's remark to me on the phone that this event was being called "Thâystock," the meditators' Woodstock.

Bells rang, introductions were made and Thich Nhat Hanh took his place on the small platform at the foot of the hill. His calm and charm radiated out over the field, and a feeling of delight cap-

Walking meditation at Spirit Rock

tured my heart. I thought about the first time I met Thây, at an ecumenical retreat in 1987 in Santa Barbara, where fifty people gathered to receive teachings from this modest Vietnamese monk. In the few short years since, his grace and wisdom had attracted thousands of followers. I was proud to be sitting here, watching history unfold. In a society where popularity is gained by flaunting one's sexuality and wealth, where war is celebrated with ticker tape parades, where we feel more and more pressure to have surgeons alter our bodies so that we can be loved, I felt a moment of deep reassurance when I looked around and saw a hillside of friends and strangers gathered in silence to be reminded in simple language about wisdom and compassion, about simply becoming who we are.

Thây's language is disarmingly simple. In/out, flower/fresh, mountain/solid, water/reflecting, space/free. This is the gatha we used during a half hour of sitting practice. One word for each in-breath, one word for each out-breath. Feeling the breath moving into the body, out of the body, feeling the breath moving deeply, feeling ourselves slowing down, feeling the wind around us and the breath inside us, seeing the flowers abundant in the fields, seeing ourselves as flowers, feeling fresh as the flowers. The effect of using the simple gatha is surprisingly profound. A wave of calm swept through the hillside of 1,200 meditators.

The day followed the usual pattern of a Day of Mindfulness. He gave a Dharma talk in a slow, calm voice. We had a break where people maintained silence as they walked into the woods or to the outhouses. We gathered for a walking meditation. A thousand people followed Thây up the pathway through the rolling California hills of tall spring grasses already golden from the drought. At the top of the hill we sat and Thây gave another talk.

We returned for lunch. People sat in quiet clusters, munching on whatever they had packed with them, and then lay in the grass or wandered in the woods. When I am around Thây I start moving more slowly, speaking more slowly, thinking more slowly. The calm sneaks up on me, like a lover who comes in the back door, knows his way around my house, and puts on the kettle.

❋

One Perfect Plum Moment Begets Another

I slowly lift my eyelids and unfold my legs
Through the half open window-door, cool evening air
rolls off the waves of grass into my lap.
The night green field and spruce/oak hedgerow
Silhouette a red to purple blue Perigord summer sunset

A moth flutters against one windowpane
nosing for a hole in the glass
never losing touch with the clear hard surface
remaining bound by the borders of the brown pine sash

The moth stops on the lower half of the windowpane
framed in the middle of the slowly changing horizon
All is calm, still.

Suddenly the moth begins anew
but after one pass along the glass
it falls back into the room straight towards me
in a swooping wabbling barrel roll dive

At the last moment it pulls out
arching back at the window
but instead it swerves out the open door
into the free night space.

—Ashley Cadwell

During the entire rest of the afternoon I sat on the hillside mesmerized by the wind blowing patterns through tall grasses. I was fascinated by the changing shapes of the coastal clouds moving through the sky. I was content watching nature be alive. More than content, I was in a state of wonder, the way I remember being as a child, fascinated by the world, finding my own place by seeing what took place around me. This is what equanimity means, I realized. Being calm enough to see, and in the act of seeing becoming more calm. I hadn't spent so many hours outdoors for quite a while and when I am outdoors I'm busy—hiking or gardening or talking. On the Day of Mindfulness, I did very little, and in the not doing, became alive.

At the end of the day, after the songs and the poetry and the announcements and the talks and the walks and the breathing, I was mostly grateful to have found a teacher who could lead me to that place of quiet where the senses take pleasure in the world. This is what interbeing is about, I remembered, in the moments of quiet appreciation of that place and the magic of nature. It is about sitting in the field and watching the wind whip the grasses the way wind whips grasses, about watching the clouds move the way clouds move, about smelling the grasses and the trees, about feeling the coolness of wind on my cheeks. I thought about Brian Swimme's hypothesis that human beings participate in completing the equation of life by being aware of the beauty that surrounds them. That nature in some way becomes complete with the self-conscious appreciation and awe that human consciousness provides. I thought about how nature with awareness is an equation for love. I remembered Thây's teaching about how trees love the sky and the sky loves the ocean and the ocean loves people and people love the sun and the sun loves the trees. That we exist in this field of love becomes entirely self-evident at moments of deep calm. We don't need to call it Buddhism or Biology or Dharma or Gaia. We need only to be still and open our senses to the world that presents itself to us moment to moment to moment.

Allan, Marion, Angelique, and I made our way back to our car and followed a long line of easy moving traffic. When we arrived at my cottage, I invited them in.

"Tea?" I offered.

We sat, slowly sipping the warm liquid, grateful for Sangha. After saying good-bye to my friends, I sat on my new couch, reading the Sunday paper.

"Remember," I told myself, "this paper was once a tree moving in the wind under a sky alive with clouds. Remember."

River Water, Market Rice

Chân Không

Anh Chan enjoys a moment with her two younger sisters

On summer mornings in Plum Village, a fine white mist covers the surrounding hillsides. Returning from walking meditation this morning, I met young Tho carrying a bucket of water to her three plum trees. Further into the orchard, I saw Kim Trang and little Thuc Hien dragging a hose out to water their trees. Here in southwestern France, plum trees flourish with only occasional watering, because the clay in the soil preserves the moisture well. The 1,250 plum trees brought to mind the many Vietnamese children in the West who sent money to purchase them, knowing that one day the dried plums would be sold to buy food and medicine for hungry children in Vietnam. Today that dream has become a reality.

I helped Tho water her trees. "Dear Tho, do you remember when you first came to Plum Village? I showed you photos of the children in the 'new economic zones' in Vietnam, and you and your sisters decided to save pocket money to help us plant ten plum trees. Do you see how your plum trees have been bearing fruit since the moment you felt a wish to help other children?" Tho turned her face toward me, her mouth forming a shy smile. How pretty she looks in her pink shirt and black trousers, just like a young girl in Vietnam. Her mother bought these traditional clothes in the Plum Village gift shop.

Tho and her family have returned to Plum Village every summer since Tho was four. The family practices mindfulness together for a month, and the children learn about Vietnamese culture. Now Tho can read and speak Vietnamese, but still she is different from the way I was

at her age, and even from the youngsters who have recently arrived from Vietnam. Whenever Tho picks up a book in French, she reads it as naturally as drinking water. But when I give her a book in Vietnamese, she looks at a few pages and then sets it aside. When Tho writes to me in Vietnamese, her letters are short, written just to please me. But when she writes to her friends in French, they go on for pages. Looking beyond Tho's shy smile, I can see that it is not possible for her to be 100 percent Vietnamese in the same way Chau is.

Chau is the daughter of a family in South Vietnam that our community has been supporting for many years. Chau's father was in a reeducation camp for more than ten years, and her mother, a public health technician, lost her job when it was discovered that her husband had worked for the nationalist regime. When Chau was only two and her brother Khang six, the family was sent to a "new economic zone," a collective farm in the jungle.

One night Chau fell ill with malaria. Her mother tied her in a sling across her back, and, balancing Khang on the front of her bicycle, pedaled to a city hospital. Halfway there, she met my sister Thanh, an old friend of hers, and Thanh wrote me about Chau's family. We were able to send them modest support, enough to help them survive. Chau's mother was able to rent a tiny house in a poor section of Saigon, barely large enough for a bed, a table, and a small stove. Every morning she sold rice porridge, and every evening she sold sweet snacks on the street. Working day and night, she had no time for her children. But with our assistance, Khang was able to attend school.

I often gaze at the photo that Chau's mother sent to me. Chau's tiny face is gaunt, and her legs thin as bamboo. The parcels we send contain medicine that can be sold for rice and vitamins for Chau and Khang. The children don't seem to gain any weight, but at least they haven't succumbed to illness like so many other children in Vietnam.

Reflecting on Khang and Chau's difficult life, my thoughts drift to the Vietnamese mothers in Europe. Like trees torn from their native soil and transplanted far away, they have struggled to create stable roots in their new countries. Tho's mother, for example, is overwhelmed by the endless paperwork she has to complete in a language she does not really understand. She works full-time to support her family, cooks dinner, washes the family's clothes, puts the children to bed, and then attends night school to try to learn French. When she gets home, no matter how tired she is, she tidies the house before going to bed. She has to be up by six in the morning to prepare breakfast and lunch for the children, and then she puts on several layers of sweaters and a pair of heavy boots to brave the snow and catch the bus to

work. She and her husband use what little time they have on the weekends to teach their children Vietnamese language and culture. Despite their efforts, Tho still reads Vietnamese hesitantly. She will never be a true Vietnamese daughter like Chau.

Every morning, Chau's mother walks along the streets of Saigon, balancing two big pots of porridge on a bamboo pole, and every evening, she sells a sweet snack, *che*. But even when she sells all that she has, there is barely enough money to buy rice, salt, firewood, coal, and vegetables. Chau's mother never has the luxury of a weekend. A day without work is truly a day without food. Even though Chau and Khang are left unattended for hours on end, they live in the cradle of Vietnamese culture, and their mother does not need to do anything to teach them the ways of our people. They learn everything by themselves. Like water in the river and rice in the market, they receive their culture every day.

The tiny shack of Khang and Chau is next door to the grand house of a Saigon University professor. Like Khang and Chau's father, the professor was also sent to a reeducation camp, and his grown children have had to support their mother and secretly preserve their father's books and papers. It was difficult to imagine how they managed to hide his books from the authorities, but then I received a letter from Khang: "Dear Aunt, I've just read *A Rose for Your Pocket*, by Thich Nhat Hanh, and it's wonderful! I felt so much love for my mother after reading it." Then, a few months later, he wrote: "Dear Aunt, I've just read *Mam Forest* and *A Taste of Earth*. They are both so good! I can't understand why such books are censored and burned."

Shortly after that, I received a letter from Chau, written in a delicate and pretty script. She began by telling me, "Dear Aunt, my mother is terribly sick. Brother Khang must now sell the porridge, or we are afraid we will lose customers. I should go and help him, but Mother is so sick I don't dare leave her alone. Aunt, my old mother is like a ripe banana hanging on the tree. She is so weak, and we are very worried!" Was this really written by a pale and skinny six-year-old girl, whose dazed eyes seem unable to grasp the harshness of her life? How could she know the beautiful folk expression "An old mother is like a ripe banana hanging on the tree"? The Vietnamese children at Plum Village have never even seen a banana tree. But when little Chau saw her mother so sick and exhausted, at once she saw the image of a banana so ripe it was about to fall from the tree. No one had to teach her this image. It was born from her experience and her insight.

Studying Vietnamese at Plum Village

Her letter continued, "Every time Mother coughs, she reminds me of the flickering wick of an oil lamp about to go out. It tears at my heart, dear Aunt!" "Flickering wick"—how could the children in Europe conjure up such an image? They have never lived by the light of an oil lamp and do not know the total darkness that descends when both oil and wick are spent. Do Vietnamese children in the West know that many children's nights in Vietnam are lit by no more than a dim, flickering oil lamp, easily extinguished by a blast of wind? Yes, Chau's mother's health—with no money, no medicine, no hospital—was like a flickering wick.

Even though she is learning Vietnamese, Tho would not be able to read Chau's letter and understand the deep meaning and feeling in her images. It is impossible for Tho to understand the terrible darkness that threatens Chau and her brother if their "lamp" goes out.

Chau's letter continued, "Every day, when I return from school, I soak the beans and begin to grate the coconut. When Khang comes home from selling porridge, we cook the sweet che together. I squeeze coconut for milk until late at night. In the morning, I get up early to heat the porridge for Khang to sell. I also chop salted pickles for him to take along. When he returns, we start to cook more porridge and che. We have no time to study.

"Before Mother got sick, I would study every evening, and then help her grate the coconut, and Khang would help her rinse the beans. When we finished, we would go next door and ask Huong if we could borrow one of her father's books. After reading *The Fragrance of Ca Mau Forest*, I loved the land of South Vietnam so dearly that I wanted to read every book by Son Nam. In Huong's library, I found a recent work by him, entitled *Nghe Harbor*, but I could only read to page thirty. The language was as bland as dried manioc roots. I couldn't swallow any more of it! No wonder it sat openly on the shelf in the living room of Huong's family. But when I read *Memoirs*, by Vu Bang, affection for the North welled within me. I am not like my friends who hate everything from the North. To reject it all because of the bad deeds of some North Vietnamese doesn't seem right, don't you agree, dear Aunt? But sometimes I wonder, does the lovely North of Vu Bang still exist? Or is the North only filled with reeducation camps, and prisoners like Father?"

It alarmed me that Chau dared to write so boldly. If this letter had been opened and examined, Chau herself would have been sent to a reeducation camp! Could Vietnamese children of the same age in Europe read such books and have such insights? I am reminded again of river water and market rice. Even without instruction, Chau receives the water and rice of her native country. Books like *A Rose for Your Pocket*, *Mam Forest*, and *Memoirs*, though hard to find in Vietnam today, are still understood and appreciated by

Plum orchard fun

children like Khang and Chau. They have the passion to read and are nourished by such books.

Tho's mother also has a copy of *The Fragrance of Ca Mau Forest*, but Tho could not read it with the same interest. She prefers to spend her time watching TV and videotapes. River water and market rice cannot be communicated just by books. Chau and Khang hear the folk songs children sing on the streets, the lullabies of village mothers, and even the gossip of women at the market. Wherever they go, Chau and Khang encounter river water and market rice. Their culture envelops them.

Today in Vietnam, the water and rice are not pure; they are mixed with sand and gravel. Pure water and rice, like good books, have been banned to make room for water and rice that make little Chau feel as if she has eaten tasteless, dry manioc root. Son Nam's writing today is not the same as when he wrote freely about his beloved country in *The Fragrance of Ca Mau Forest*. If Chau wants to taste pure water and fra-

grant, delicious rice, she has to carefully separate out the pebbles, manioc, and rotten grains. Mixed in with the fine beauties of our home-land—ripe bananas, golden plum flowers, and village mothers' lullabies—are the hardened, cold faces of the communist cadres in their yellow uniforms. Their rough tone makes their Vietnamese sound like a foreign language. These people treat a kind, talented scholar like Huong's father worse than a common pickpocket, so how could their water and rice not be polluted?

Khang wrote to me describing his neighbor's second arrest: "Twelve cadres arrived at 2:00 in the morning and searched every corner of the professor's house, while two others stood guard in front. I could hear Huong speaking to the cadres, while the professor sat in meditation, as quiet as Buddha, with a half-smile on his lips. Even as they led him out with handcuffs at 8:00

a.m., his expression was calm and serene. My heart was filled with love and admiration. You know, Aunt, my own father is brave like the professor. That is why he is still in prison after twelve years." One only has to open one's eyes to see that the market is still abundant with rice and the rivers are still flowing with clear water. Even rice mixed with gravel still has some delicious, pure rice in it, enough to feed those who know how to select the pure rice and stay in full awareness in their beautiful homeland.

Books like *Mam Forest*, *The Fragrance of Ca Mau Forest*, and *Memoirs* are available in Europe, but do the Vietnamese children raised here know how to savor every line, and appreciate the beauty of each word? I feel ill-at-ease when I think of the many refugee children drawn in by violent scenes on TV whenever they have some free time. These youngsters will never have the occasion to watch the dear professor face the twelve violent cadres with a serene smile. They will never have the chance to hear village mothers sing soft lullabies to their babies on a hot afternoon, nor will they hear the inspiring stories of those sent to "new economic zones" or imprisoned in "reeducation camps" who continued to be calm and brave. Even if the professor manages to escape and write a book about his experiences, it is unlikely that youngsters overseas will care to read his book. No matter how much time Tho's mother devotes to teaching Vietnamese to her children, it is impossible for the children to be in touch with the wondrous reality of Vietnam. For them, it is just an unfamiliar distant land.

I breathed deeply. At least I have a few photographs of the poor children in the new economic zones that I can share with the children who come to Plum Village. And there are the plum trees to help connect them with children their own age in Vietnam. Looking at the photographs, they can see that they resemble the children in Vietnam more than they look like their classmates in school, even though the children in Vietnam are skinny and live in palm-leaf huts. Every summer, Vietnamese children from all over Europe, North America, and Australia come to Plum Village to discover the richness and the depth of their parents' language, poetry, music, and culture.

I smiled, remembering Tho's Swiss teacher's amazement after reading this essay by her: "A fragrant rose and a heap of garbage are two sides of one living reality. Looking deeply into a rose, I can see the garbage. Looking deeply into the garbage, I can see a rose. It will bloom very soon. When I look anywhere, I see flowers and garbage deeply interconnected. This is necessary for life to be." The Swiss teacher tried to visit Tho's family to understand how such a little girl could have such deep thoughts. It is because Tho visits Plum Village every summer. Although Tho may not be as fully Vietnamese as Chau, she will be able to learn many lessons that children in Vietnam cannot because of poverty and the lack of freedom. Any child who comes to Plum Village can learn from Thây Nhat Hanh about non-duality and other important aspects of life. And refugee children in the West receive the benefits of nutritious food, freedom, and openness, and will grow up to be healthy offshoots of the "tree of Vietnam."

Preparing for the Full Moon Festival

✳
Reflections

Plum Village is a fascinating place. It has culture, religion, and many other things. Dharma talks are cool. One can express their innermost feelings without being shy or embarrassed about their problems or their love and interest. But in the Lower Hamlet, it is quite hard to understand or learn the Vietnamese language because the grownups go into such depth that a lot of the words are hard to understand. This problem would be easy to solve, but it would mean causing interruptions and disturbances to the others.

There is another problem. The young people in the Lower Hamlet are not good at the Vietnamese language, so they cannot really contribute or go into depth to express their innermost feelings. It is a shame because they will be too shy and scared to speak out because of the mistakes that they might make.

—Teo, 13-year-old Vietnamese boy living in England

✳

I would like to write in Vietnamese, but I know that the words would be spelled wrong. I should learn more Vietnamese because I am Vietnamese. I am sorry. More than anything, I wish to thank Thây for creating Plum Village. If Thây didn't exist, Plum Village wouldn't exist. Plum Village and Thây have changed me a lot. I have learned to calm myself down. I used to be a wild child. I still am a bit, but now I am able to control some of my temper. I have learned to be aware of what I am doing, to be mindful. I am still working to improve on it. Meditation is good. During sitting meditation I am aware of my breathing. Walking meditation, hugging meditation, and eating meditation have all been helpful for me. Dharma talks are great even though I sometimes don't understand them. But the parts I understand help me. Being in Plum Village has helped me a lot.

—Ti, 11-year-old Vietnamese girl living in England

The professor who was arrested cannot teach the children in Vietnam about flowers and garbage. Twenty years ago, the cadres who arrested him might have been like flowers, but because of their victory over the Americans, they have become like garbage, filled with arrogance. What about the beautiful flowers, like the professor or the father of Khang and Chau? Once they get out of jail and are able to emigrate to a free country, will they still be fresh? Will they continue to cultivate their qualities to blossom and give joy, peace, and inspiration to millions of young Vietnamese flowers? Or will the easy life in the West draw them slowly into forgetfulness? Now the professor is not there to teach Khang, so he only sees the communist cadres as garbage to be thrown away. No one is there to teach him the ways to transform garbage into flowers.

It is so sad to see that thirty years of war followed by eighteen years of dictatorship have transformed the minds of the Vietnamese people into yet another war zone. In the past, Vietnam as a nation had many people who embodied great virtues—people who knew the arts of humility, deep listening, and looking deeply. Such enlightened persons are now difficult to find.

Seeds from the Bodhi tree in India have been planted throughout the world. Because of different soil and water conditions, each bodhi tree grows a little differently. Some are tall; some are short. But each one contains the essence of the original bodhi tree. Now I see that if Vietnamese children living overseas are lucky enough to have parents who live in awareness, they will thrive, even if they take on a new shape. They will be lovely Vietnamese trees, contributors to the garden of humanity, thriving among the mountains of Switzerland, in France with its rich heritage, in the lowlands of Holland, the snowy lands of Denmark, Sweden, Norway, and Finland, the wealth and talent of Germany, and the lands of opportunity of America and Australia. For the first time I can see that Vietnam is not just the small dragon-shaped country on the South China Sea. It is now the whole world, extending from the Americas to Europe, and all the way down to Australia.

The challenge is to encourage Vietnamese parents to preserve the beautiful part of the culture of their native land and pass it on to their children. How can I encourage them to give themselves more time to cultivate flowers in themselves and in their children and to cultivate our culture's spiritual depth before everyone in the family gets caught up in selfish concerns? Parents must show an interest in what their children are learning at school, while also sharing with them the delightful customs and traditions of the new land. Looking deeply into each new habit and tradition with their children, they can learn to appreciate the best things about the West and keep them away from the worst habits. Sharing in this way will allow the children to receive and love the culture of their homeland, and plant it intelligently in the rich, new soil. Parents and children can look deeply together to see why the ancestors took the time to welcome the blooming of a single flower and celebrate the full moon. They can learn to feel within themselves the continuation of their ancestors. They can find ways to stay in touch with those who have no food and no freedom, and ways to celebrate their gratitude to teachers, friends, and all beings. Living in awareness, parents will not say or do things that will cause their children to lose faith in their own people. Then there will be hope that the children will want to continue their heritage and study Vietnamese, as they study French, German, and English. In this way, the children will see and understand the joys and pains of their people's 4,000-year history.

No matter how great an effort Tho's mother makes, Tho will be different from Chau. Each girl has her own unique beauty. It is true that Tho looks like an elegant pine from Switzerland, but her dark eyes, shy smile, and silky black hair are like the sweet rice and coconut milk of her parents' Vietnam. Her way of speaking, walking, and greeting friends are the fruits of the love and guidance she has received from her parents, grandparents, uncles and aunts, her ancestral heritage.

Suddenly, my thoughts were interrupted by the sweet voice of young Thanh Tuyen, "Who wants bean cakes, who wants coconut cakes?" She is carrying a platter of Vietnamese cakes, calling out like a street vendor. In her brown blouse and black trousers, slightly wrinkled from her noontime nap, Thanh Tuyen sounds just like a vendor from North Vietnam selling cakes along the streets of Saigon. Though her parents are from the South and speak in a southern accent, as a young child in Vietnam Thanh Tuyen often heard vendors from the North. Every summer when she visits Plum Village, she is invited to use her voice

Dancing to traditional Vietnamese music in Dharma Nectar Hall

to sell the traditional cakes. Thanks to the presence of Plum Village, she has a chance to recollect and preserve the image of her homeland. Hopefully in every region where there are Vietnamese people, places like Plum Village will be created where Vietnamese children can come and give new life to these fading images of their homeland.

Every tradition has its jewels. Now, amidst worldwide migration and diaspora, the riches of a multicultural civilization can spring forth. We do our best at Plum Village to be a part of this by encouraging Vietnamese and all other guests to keep one foot firmly planted in their traditional culture and one foot in their new one. Together we can help create a beautiful garden of humanity for the next century.

Beginning Anew

Annabel Laity

We can see the great effect of a simple ceremony like Beginning Anew in alleviating suffering and preventing disharmony. In India in the sixth century B.C.E., monks and nuns practiced the *Pavarana* ceremony at the Full Moon at the end of the rainy-season retreat and also in connection with the *uposatha* days when the precepts were recited. Sometimes Pavarana is translated as "invitation," because we invite others to tell us of our shortcomings. At Plum Village, we translate Pavarana as "Beginning Anew." Chinese translators 1,500 years ago used that translation. Disclosing or uncovering our regrets, our hurts, and our shortcomings helps us begin again. Monks and nuns have continued practicing this ceremony to the present day before the twice-monthly precept recitation ceremony.

The ceremony begins with the head of the community revealing his or her own shortcomings, and is followed by other members of the community doing the same, according to their seniority. A monk or nun kneels before another member of the community and invites that person to reveal his or her failures. The person requested to do this may not want to, but agrees to do so because the person kneeling before him has requested it three times. If the community member is skillful, he or she will reveal the faults in a nonrecriminating way and may also give the monk or nun some encouragement at the same time. The effectiveness of the ceremony depends on our depth of commitment to listening and speaking wholeheartedly. If we do not practice deep listening and wholehearted speaking, someone might, for example, reveal faults without feeling remorse or in a way that recriminates another member of the community.

Transformation Hall altar, with brush painting by Mike Kline

In fact, a religious community is a family in which we do not hesitate to be guided by those older than we, if we know they are guiding us out of love and concern for our well-being and the well-being of the community. We listen carefully when we are corrected and think carefully before reacting. We never answer back immediately. We

Ý THỨC EM MỤT TRỜI TỎ RẠNG

(My Awareness is the Shining Sun)

Cham rai, tu do

Thich Nhat Hanh

Thức dậy hôm nay em thấy trời xanh Chắp

tay em cám ơn đời mầu nhiệm Cho

em hai mươi bốn giờ tinh khôi Cho em bầu trời bao

la Mặt trời lên cao rừng cây ý thức Mặt trời

lên cao... rừng cây vương nắng chan hòa. Em

đi ngang qua đồng hoa hướng dương Hằng vạn bông hoa

ngoảnh nhìn về phương đông chói sáng. Ý thức em mặt

trời tỏ rạng Bàn tay em gieo hạt cho mùa sang

năm. 1) Biển động tai em nghe tiếng triều dâng Xôn xao mây
2) Đất mẹ cho em hương quế tần ô Tía tô rau

bốn phương trời lồng lộng Quê hương thân yêu ngát hồ sen
húng rau ngò mầu nhiệm Mai đầy xanh tươi núi đồi quê

thơm Quê hương hàng dừa ven sông Ruộng đồng vươn vai Cười theo bông
hương Mai đầy lộc đời lên nhanh Ngọt lời ca dao Trần gian vui

lúa Ruộng đồng vươn vai cười mưa vui nắng trăm mùa. (Đất..
hát Ngọt lời ca dao mầu xanh đưa bước chân người.

say silently or aloud, "Thank you for your advice. I will consider it carefully." Then, joining our palms, we bow our head. In a family with small children, the best way to guide the children is usually not to shout or hit, but to point out with a smile and a caress how to do better, taking the opportunity at the same time to talk about some of the child's strong points.

Traditionally, the Pavarana ceremony was not for lay families. But why should they not enjoy all the benefits that monks and nuns enjoy, even if it means modifying the ceremony in certain respects? The same modifications may even make the ceremony more effective for monks and nuns. The monks and nuns in Plum Village practice very much in a way that lay families can practice.

Once a week, if we possibly can, the whole family or the whole community comes together. It is good to choose a day when people do not feel too much pressure from homework or work. Lying-down meditation, either listening to soothing music or in silence, can be a very useful way to relax before Beginning Anew.

✳

Beginning Anew Ceremony

The "Beginning Anew" ceremony that Thây has given us is a real jewel. During one Beginning Anew Ceremony at Plum Village, a senior student spoke very openly and even lightly about things she had done or said in an unskillful way. Her acceptance of herself gave me a feeling of spaciousness. We all make mistakes. Speaking out about our mistakes strips them of their heaviness.

At first, I felt a little nervous, not knowing what would come up for me. I pondered how to speak out in the best way. It is amazing how frightening it can be to speak openly about regret or feeling hurt. The latter is quite difficult for me. But as the ceremony proceeded, I could feel the air clearing. To witness so many hearts opening like flowers, to see people being so sincere, authentic, loving, and honest, touched me deeply.

Each Beginning Anew session I have attended has ended with a room filled with love and warmth. Beginning Anew brings about more than even the air clearing up. We rediscover how woven together we are. Beginning Anew is the backbone of the Sangha, a living example of Thây's teaching about how to transform our "garbage" into a flower.

—Eveline Beumkes

Arrange a fresh flower in a vase and put it in the middle of the circle. Do your best to have everyone who lives with you there. Enjoy your breathing and your concentration as you wait for someone to begin the ceremony. We begin by "flower-watering," pointing out the encouraging points of the others present. We always speak the truth. This is not a time for mere flattery. Everyone has strong points which, with awareness, we can see.

The ceremony can be in three stages: encouraging the wonderful things we observe in each other, expressing our regrets for our own shortcomings, and expressing our hurts and difficulties. When you are ready to speak, join your palms to indicate that you are ready. The others present will join their palms to show their assent.

Then you rise from your seat and approach the flower, which you take in your hands and return to your seat. Then you begin to speak, your words reflecting the freshness and beauty of the flower you hold.

When you have finished, stand up slowly and return the flower to its vase. While one person holds the flower, no one else has the right to speak. We allow people as much time as they need to speak encouragingly to each other. Then we can begin to express our regrets for what we have done to hurt others. The Beginning Anew ceremony is an excellent opportunity for us to recall a moment earlier in the week when we said or did something that may have caused damage-and to put it right. Later on, if you feel ready, you take the flower and invite others to let you know of your own shortcomings of which you have been unaware. "I know I have faults that I am not aware of. Please help me, brothers and sisters, by revealing them to me." Sometimes people are too worried about hurting our feelings, so we need to insist firmly that we want to hear our shortcomings. That is why traditionally one repeats this request three times.

Listening meditation is the way to enlightenment practiced by the Bodhisattva Avalokitesvara. We listen without expecting to reply. We listen so deeply and attentively that the speaker's suffering can be transformed just by our listening. To sit in a circle of people who are all practicing listening is truly to experience meditation. The speaker is helped by that meditation. Everyone is one of the thousand arms of the bodhisattva. The bodhisattva is made up of us all.

We close the ceremony with a song, by holding hands and breathing for a minute, or with hugging meditation. The closing should be warm, to help us feel light and relieved even if we have only taken the first step toward healing, because having begun, we have confidence that we can continue.

The Six Principles of Harmony

Annabel Laity

After seeing how Anuruddha, Kimbila, and Nandiya lived in harmony together, the Buddha arrived at the Six Concords, principles for being happy together.

The first is "the body as a principle of harmony." In a community, we try to learn how to be both individuals and community members at the same time. In the West we stress individualism. At Plum Village we are trying to learn ways to diminish our individualism while, at the same time, learning how to practice in a way that is creative and full of our own initiative.

We share common space in a community, but we have to take into account that we are many different bodies. Everyone is a member of the family, but each person is responsible for looking after his own health. We don't want to become a burden on the community, so we try our best to stay healthy. If someone is a little sick, everyone feels a little sick at the same time. When someone catches a cold, the whole community worries and gives advice.

We also learn to breathe together. Everyone's breath is a little different. If we are sensitive to another person, we can breathe with him or her. Sometimes, rather than talking with someone, we just breathe together. Those who work with the dying know how to harmonize their breath with the person who is dying. This can be a wonderful practice.

The Buddha's second principle, "the sharing principle," is about sharing material things with the community. The Buddha observed that when the monks returned from their almsrounds, they would always set aside some food for the monk who was last to return.

In the larger community of the Buddha, there was a monk who shared everything he had, even a glass of water. The other monks were impressed by this and told the Buddha, who replied, "He was not always this way. In a past life, he was a king who never shared anything. One day, he desired some special porridge with rice, curds, honey, and sesame seeds, and he thought, If I

Plum Village nuns living in harmony

make this porridge in my castle, others will want some, so I'd better take the ingredients to the forest and cook the porridge there.

"Some gods saw what he was doing and disguised themselves as beggars in order to ask him for some of his porridge. At that time, people ate off of leaves, so the gods went to a special tree with huge leaves, and picked one large leaf each. Along the road, the gods smelled the porridge and went to the king. 'We were just walking by,' they began, but the king interrupted: 'Why are you walking past here?'

✳

The Five Wonderful Precepts

First Precept

Aware of the suffering caused by the destruction of life, I vow to cultivate compassion and learn ways to protect the lives of people, animals, plants, and minerals. I am determined not to kill, not to let others kill, and not to condone any act of killing in the world, in my thinking, and in my way of life.

Second Precept

Aware of the suffering caused by exploitation, social injustice, stealing, and oppression, I vow to cultivate loving kindness and learn ways to work for the well-being of people, animals, plants, and minerals. I vow to practice generosity by sharing my time, energy, and material resources with those who are in real need. I am determined not to steal and not to possess anything that should belong to others. I will respect the property of others, but I will prevent others from profiting from human suffering or the suffering of other species on Earth.

Third Precept

Aware of the suffering caused by sexual misconduct, I vow to cultivate responsibility and learn ways to protect the safety and integrity of individuals, couples, families, and society. I am determined not to engage in sexual relations without love and a long-term commitment. To preserve the happiness of myself and others, I am determined to respect my commitments and the commitments of others. I will do everything in my power to protect children from sexual abuse and to prevent couples and families from being broken by sexual misconduct.

Fourth Precept

Aware of the suffering caused by unmindful speech and the inability to listen to others, I vow to cultivate loving speech and deep listening in order to bring joy and happiness to others and relieve others of their suffering. Knowing that words can create happiness or suffering, I vow to learn to speak truthfully, with words that inspire self-confidence, joy, and hope. I am determined not to spread news that I do not know to be certain and not to criticize or condemn things of which I am not sure. I will refrain from uttering words that can cause division or discord, or that can cause the family or the community to break. I will make all efforts to reconcile and resolve all conflicts, however small.

Fifth Precept

Aware of the suffering caused by unmindful consumption, I vow to cultivate good health, both physical and mental, for myself, my family, and my society by practicing mindful eating, drinking, and consuming. I vow to ingest only items that preserve peace, well-being, and joy in my body, in my consciousness, and in the collective body and consciousness of my family and society. I am determined not to use alcohol or any other intoxicant or to ingest foods or other items that contain toxins, such as certain TV programs, magazines, books, films, and conversations. I am aware that to damage my body or my consciousness with these poisons is to betray my ancestors, my parents, my society, and future generations. I will work to transform violence, fear, anger, and confusion in myself and in society by practicing a diet for myself and for society. I understand that a proper diet is crucial for self-transformation and for the transformation of society.

"They replied, 'We are going to Vaisali,' and the king interrupted again: 'This is the wrong way to Vaisali. Go back in the other direction immediately!'

"Then one of the beggars said, 'We're extremely hungry. We haven't eaten for a long time. Can you give us a serving of your porridge?'

"The king said, 'Okay, but you cannot use those big leaves. Go and pick some smaller leaves first.'

"When they returned with smaller leaves, the king gave them each a tiny portion of porridge, and then he served himself the rest. Immediately one of the gods turned himself into a dog and urinated right in the king's porridge. The gods ate their small portions happily and told the king, 'If you don't share, things are not worth having.' From that time on," the Buddha said, "the king learned to share. In fact, he became the most generous person in the kingdom."

The third principle of harmony is practicing the same precepts. At Plum Village, we ask that everyone who joins the community keep the Five Precepts.

When we work in the plum orchard or the garden, for example, we are very aware of the First Precept—not to kill. We try not to use products that will result in killing or come from killing. To do this, we need to take more time. But if we know how to live simply, we will have the time. The slugs are really a problem, so every day we pick them up and transport them in a tin can to someplace where they won't eat the vegetables. The Five Wonderful Precepts are necessary for the wholesomeness of the community.

The fourth principle of harmony has speech as its basis. Much of our speech is habitual—it comes from things we have said before or have heard others say. When we were children, our parents repeated certain things over and over, and their habits have become a part of our own way of speaking. We need to develop new harmonious patterns of speech. Anuruddha and the other two monks told the Buddha that before they said anything they would ask themselves, "If I say this, will it make my two brothers happy?" That has to do with breaking our negative patterns of speech. If we stop and follow our breathing, there is a kind of renewal, and a new kind of speaking comes out. Before speaking, we ask ourselves, "Will it make the other person happy? Will it help the other members of the community?"

The fifth principle, harmony of views, may be the most important. We have to learn to tone down our individualism. We have strong views and deep feelings. When we hear someone speak, we usually react, "That is what I think, so it must be right," or "That is not what I think, so it must be wrong." In a community, when someone offers an idea, we need to listen deeply and take what has been said seriously. If someone else disagrees, we try to find ways that take both points of view into account.

Sharing views includes sharing our experience in the practice. It is important not just to share positive things that are happening to us, but our mistakes as well, asking others for help when needed. If we have a good experience, we shouldn't think, I'm more advanced than the others. Maybe they're not quite up to hearing this yet. We share it with them in the best way we can.

Even though it is true that the essence of what is happening to us can never be described in words, words are our vehicle. When the Buddha sat under the Bodhi tree and reached enlightenment, for seven weeks he did not know what to say. He felt he had nothing to communicate. It was only when he came into contact with the five ascetics and felt their suffering deeply that the words came to him to describe what he had experienced, and he was able to formulate the Four Noble Truths, the Twelve Links of Interdependent Origination, and the Middle Way. The Middle Way was an obvious teaching to present to those practicing extreme asceticism. It did not arise

Listening to Thay's Dharma talk, simultaneously translated into many languages

from the Buddha having a certain view. It came from seeing how the wrong view of the ascetics was leading them to suffer. In a Dharma discussion, when we present our ideas on the practice, it is partly to learn ways to talk about our experience that are helpful to ourselves and others.

The sixth principle of harmony has the mind as its basis. We use our mind, our thinking, to help others in the community. It is as if we keep a file on everyone else. We see what brings them joy and what causes them to suffer. If someone has some physical suffering, we keep that in our minds. If they tell us a story about their past, that becomes part of our file. Gradually we learn more and more about each person, and we are able to see how we can practice meditation to love them more. That is how we keep the harmony by means of the mind. Just as Ananda always kept the welfare of the Buddha in his mind, we always keep in mind the welfare of all the other members of our community.

Precious Jewel

Jina van Hengel

Every New Year's Day in some countries in Asia, monks and nuns write their last wills and testament. They light incense, sit quietly, following their breathing and looking deeply at birth and death, and think *Soon it will be the New Year. What kind of will should I write?*

What can we inherit? What can we pass on? What kind of treasure are we? Over time we receive many things, enjoy them, share them with others, and pass them on. We especially want to pass on what is most precious, so we look after those things most carefully. Whatever we receive, whatever we are—our robes, bowl, lamps, body, mind, feelings, emotions, understanding, love, and support—are all part and parcel of the precious jewel we want to pass on.

We want this heritage to go to its rightful heirs. Normally our family members are considered to be the rightful heirs, but what is it that makes an heir rightful? To me, one who is lacking in whatever is to be given is what makes him or her a rightful heir. There is a famous story about a shepherd in France who planted trees. He had lost his wife and son, and so he spent his time gathering the healthiest acorns in the forest and planting them in barren, deserted areas where nothing would grow and no one lived. Carrying a stick with a metal point, he made little holes in the ground and planted an acorn in each one. As years passed, trees sprang up and soon the barren land was transformed into a green, fertile oasis that became a national park.

For the universe to be whole, no one should lack what is essential. If food is lacking, we give food. If shelter is lacking, we give shelter. If love is lacking, we give love.

It is easy to love someone lovable. He is lovable because he already has love. He is love. But those who do not have love are the ones who need it. They ought to be the rightful heirs of our love. Someone who has love and is happy is like a beautiful landscape that we enjoy entering. Someone who has no love, who is sad or angry, is like a barren landscape where nothing will grow and no one wants to enter. However, that barren

Chanting about Avalokitesvara, the bodhisattva of compassion

land is like that because we are like this, because we turn away from it. Let us not turn away from it, but approach it, and plant acorns there so that it will transform itself into a fresh and fragrant oasis that offers peace and joy to all.

A tiny little acorn has the totality of the tree in it. The same is true of us. We inherited from our parents their whole being—including their parents, teachers, friends, and environment, everyone

STANDING LIKE A TREE

Lively

Betsy Rose

Standing like a tree with my roots dug down, my branches wide and open. Come down the rain, come down the sun, come down the fruit to the heart that is open to be... (standing)

and everything that made them, as well as everyone and everything that made our parents' teachers, friends, and parents, and their parents, teachers, friends, and so on—and that jewel is in us in its totality. We are the receiver of the heritage of the whole universe, and we are also the one who passes it on, day and night, without stopping. When we transform something negative in us into something more wholesome, we do it for everyone, and we make everyone else's transformation easier.

Once we know who our heirs are, we naturally become mindful and take good care of our heritage, our universal jewel. Our parents, grandparents, ancestors, teachers, friends, and everything that was, is, and will be are in their totality in us, and we are in our totality in everything that ever was, is, and will be. Seeing this, we understand what can be inherited and what we are passing on. Happy continuation.

Wedding at Plum Village

Therese Fitzgerald

Arnie and I were married at Plum Village in August 1989, but the seeds of our marriage were sown and watered most crucially two years earlier. When Thây and Sister Chân Không arrived in the United States for their 1987 visit, we were on the verge of separation. "Perhaps our differences are too great," I told them. They listened attentively while I recounted some of the differences. After moments of silence, Thây said, lovingly, "Be patient with Arnie." Sister Chân Không smiled and said with a twinkle in her eye, "You belong together...for many people." Later we met with them and they said similar things to us both. And, most importantly, I watched how loving and patient Thây was with Arnie, how he touched him so gently, full of appreciation.

Over the next two years, our lives became one. During the Plum Village summer session of 1989, I was working to arrange the details of another wedding by Thây, when Arnie suggested that we be married also. I conveyed this to Thây, adding that my own preference was to wait until I was less exhausted. I had been working extremely hard organizing the summer retreat. I remember glistening with perspiration during this conversation as I knelt beside Thây, who was sitting at his desk upstairs by the window in the Upper Hamlet main house. "Sister Chân Không will find an auspicious time for you," he said smilingly. Then he held out his arms, and we practiced hugging meditation in celebration of Arnie's and my clear commitment. I felt welcomed home to myself in that embrace!

On the morning of our wedding, Arnie and I arose in the misty dawn and walked from our tent at the far end of the woods to bathe and dress for the ceremony. The ceremony began with outdoor walking meditation along the sunflower fields and into the forest. It was a special delight to sit in a circle with longtime Dharma friends and sing "Breathing In, Breathing Out," and other songs of practice. During the ceremony, Thây gave us "The Five Awarenesses" to observe and recite in support of our life of cultivating

Arnie and Therese enjoying Lazy Day at Plum Village

understanding and love. Then, Arnie and I exchanged personal vows that we had written for each other:

Dear Therese, sweet, radiant bodhisattva,
You are my inspiration, my teacher.
Your sweet demeanor and selfless, charitable soul
encourage and support me
and give me hope for our future.

I vow always to cherish you
as an honored guest and friend and lover.
I vow to be open, loving, firm, and constant for
you, by you, and with you
to help us both grow in kindness and mindful-
ness, love and understanding.

I am happy to say in front of the Buddha,
the Dharma, and the Sangha
that I love you
and I am delighted, thrilled, to marry you,
here, today
and to re-marry you each moment for the rest of
our lives.

Precious Arnie,
I promise always to honor and respect you,
always to try to understand you
and give you what you need to flourish and be
happy.

Trusting in your goodness,
relaxing in your kindness,
basking in your brightness,
I vow to cherish and care for you every day for
the rest of our life.
I promise to concentrate on the seeds of joy and
generosity in my alayavijñana.

Your steady kindness and clarity throughout these
intimate, intense years have helped me to plight
my troth and vow to join truths with you every
day for the rest of our life.

Together with good friends and teachings, we will
cherish each other and enhance the lives of peo-
ple, animals, and plants. May we continue to nur-
ture each other and enhance this wondrous life
that has presented you to me.

After the ceremony, we emerged from the eighteenth-century stone meditation hall, into a cool morning to have a breakfast of fresh homemade muffins and tarts. Then the community gathered for a Dharma discussion on the Five Awarenesses, followed by a Vietnamese banquet. Since that time, feeling so assured of each other's and the Sangha's love and caring support, our energies have been one.

Sunflower Song

Martin Pitt

As I was walking alone one morning,
birds were waking and the cows were yawning.
I passed through a wood and on the other side,
a field of sunflowers opened wide.
A bright yellow field opened wide.

And from those sunlit flowers I'd found
came the most enchanting sound.
And I still remember those mournful words—
the most beautiful voice that I'd ever heard.

CHORUS:
    It was a sunflower—
    black face in a sea of black faces
    She sang to me—
    bright yellow hair in the morning breeze
    Sunflower—how silently she sang.

And the sunflower said with a tear in her eye,
"Kindly, sir, can you tell me why
we've noticed the rain that falls from the clouds
is not the same as we knew?
For it was once so clear
but now it's acid water we fear.
And if it's not too much
could you please bring back the rain that we
knew?
Could you please bring back the water we once
knew?"

CHORUS

And the sunflower said with a wave of her hair,
"Kindly, sir, can you tell me where
the wind that blows from across the fields
is not from the place we once knew?
For there was once such a beautiful breeze,
but now these gases poison our leaves.
And if it's not too much
could you please bring back the wind that we
knew?
Could you please bring back the air that we once
knew?"

CHORUS

And the sunflower said with an innocent sigh,
"Kindly, sir, can you tell me why
the soil that holds our roots in the ground
is not as rich as before?
For the powder the farmer spreads with machines
is washed by the rainfall down to the streams.
And it poisons our cousins, the fish and the trees.
Could you please bring back the soil we knew?
Could you please bring back the earth that we
once knew?"

CHORUS

As I was walking alone one morning,
birds were waking and the cows were yawning.
I passed through a wood and on the other side
a field of sunflowers opened wide.
A bright yellow field opened wide.

TASTE AND SEE

Lilting

Betsy Rose

Oh— taste, taste and see— how good is the fruit that

falls from the tree. Oh— taste, taste and see— how good is the fruit of the

gar-den.
1. Taste the sun, stored in the skin: Fla-vor of fire and of
2. Taste the rain, soaked through the flesh: It lin-gers so sweet on the

pas - sion. Taste the stars that dwell at the core: Seeds of our joy and com-
tongue.—— Taste the earth, the bo - dy of life: Dark and— rich and—

pas - sion. Oh...
strong— Oh...

Stopping to Thank

Chân Huong Nghiêm

My stay at Plum Village in the past three years has helped me greatly in understanding, appreciating, and accepting myself, which in turn has helped me to understand, appreciate, and accept other people. My experience with the practice of looking deeply has strengthened my faith and confidence in the teachings of the Buddha and the presence of a practicing community. The contentment I find with my lifestyle and its present course is much more fulfilled. A basic, much-needed prerequisite to the practice of looking deeply is the willingness to stop. Stop what? Stop the urge to beat time; stop the tendency to focus on the future and forget the intermediate milestones; stop the habit of letting worries and sorrows overtake my life; stop in order to take a breather, to reconsider my needs and refocus my energies, directing them more appropriately.

Coming to Plum Village was my action of stopping, to give myself some time to look at my past, to take an inventory of my needs, weaknesses, and strengths, and to redirect the course of my life toward something more meaningful and beneficial. My first three months were like living in a fantasy land with few worries and much, much freedom. Many beautiful memories of daily activities such as learning to make tofu, to cook (take my word, disastrous moments were plentiful!), or times when we had to relocate the snails and slugs from our vegetable gardens to the deep woods, or quiet times watching the little kittens grow up, play with each other, explore their new terrain. I was pleasantly surprised to find that in strengthening my interactions with people in Plum Village, I had indirectly nourished my family roots. I can now understand each of my family members better. I can see the love and care they have deserved and have been giving me all these years. This newly discovered confidence has grounded me, enabling me to take control of my life with more clarity.

Under the linden tree

Every summer at Plum Village, the community celebrates Rose Festival to honor and appreciate our mothers and fathers

The practice of looking deeply helps me in dealing with sorrows that run deep. I find that this practice is much more effective if I look deeply into little irritations and small anxieties each day. I know how my mind can trick me into blaming things on external conditions or other people. By looking deeply, I personally know that not everything taught by the Buddha or Thây can be implemented exactly the same way for everyone in all circumstances!

The practice of looking deeply has helped me appreciate the beautiful, nourishing parts of my life. It has also helped me work on "recycling" internal difficulties into more beneficial energy. I find myself starting to truly enjoy each moment of practice (although it is still not continuous), truly appreciating the gifts of nature and the presence of a practicing community. I took these for granted in the past, and now I find that I have much more to be happy about, much more to live for, much more just to be!

Thank you for this opportunity to share my experience in the practice with you. This was in itself an exercise in looking deeply in order to be able to convey the fruits of my practice to you.

Transforming Life and Death

Metta Lepousé

I had an uneventful early childhood. I grew up on a farm in France with loving parents. I quarreled a lot with my two brothers, and, when I was six, I had a little sister whom I cherished a lot, and still do.

However, when I turned nine or ten, huge waves of sadness started rushing over me, and I would find myself crying inexplicably no matter what I was doing. I felt that life was too difficult, and I imagined death as a very peaceful place. I tried to kill myself, although in very childish ways—holding my breath as long as I could, putting my head under water in a bucket, and so on. As I grew up, I became more sophisticated. I tried to hang myself with a curtain string. Then finally I got the idea of swallowing pills. That sent me to the hospital and my mom found out about my illness. She understood that only a drastic change would keep me alive and she gave me a plane ticket to Africa. I had not imagined this possibility, and I gratefully accepted, beginning a life of travel that was to continue for ten years. After that, I became tired of traveling and found no interest in life again. I was seriously thinking of committing suicide when I met the spiritual path, and right away I understood that killing myself would not solve my problems. Still, I was very attracted to death.

Then one day I met a Chinese master. When he saw me he said, "Are you a ghost or a human being?"

"A human being."

"Who is trying to kill herself all the time then?"

Shantum and Marie taking a rest from the very full summer schedule

I passed out on the spot. So intense was my fascination with death, he had been able to see it just by looking at me.

I have been practicing ever since, and seven years ago I encountered Thây. During my first summer at Plum Village, I was interested in something Thây often repeats: "Nothing is created, nothing is destroyed." What about death then?

✳ Mindfulness in Prison

After thirteen years of formal meditation, I decided that the practice of mindfulness is the tradition I wish to follow, and I incorporated the practice of mindfulness into my weekly meditation class at a juvenile prison in Topeka, Kansas. Even though I have not mastered the element of joy, several young men have commented on my patience. Others have asked such questions as, "Why do you want to transform anger?" They do not seem to connect anger to violence and suffering. I seem to run into a barrier each time one of them raises this kind of question.

One Friday evening, I was teaching meditation to a new group of young men, drawing heavily on my experience from a retreat I had just attended with Thich Nhat Hanh. One large, well-built young man came in late, grumbling. I told him that I could see he was angry, and asked if he would like to talk about it. He said that he was angry at having to be in this group. I used the occasion of anger to work on anger; getting into breathing, calming the body, and allowing ourselves to smile. It was a beautiful opportunity to speak of not pushing our anger away, but observing it and allowing our understanding to grow and transform the anger into a more affirming energy.

Twenty-minutes into the session, this man commented to me, "I'm not angry anymore." I thanked him and we went on to practice two brief guided meditations.

—Daniel McMahon

Isn't it a place where everything stops and disappears? So I put my question to Thây in the bell as we do at Plum Village, and Thây gave a Dharma talk one morning addressing my question. I felt liberated, free from a lifelong illusion. Life and death happen in every moment. Death does not mean an end, but rather a transformation—elements breaking up and being reassembled in different shapes and beings, eternally old, eternally new. Continuation, like ocean, mist, clouds, rain, and rivers. Cessation exists but is not synonymous with death. Cessation can be in each breath. It is about stopping mental formations. It can be done here and now. When the church bell or the telephone rings, I stop, and in a way I die. No need to carry on the endless burden. Putting it down, I rest totally for a few seconds.

Realizing this truth and being able to practice cessation has transformed my life. The ghost in me has been defeated. I am becoming more of a human being every day thanks to this wonderful and compassionate Dharma master we call Thây. In fact, in the past two years I married a wonderful American man and gave birth to a beautiful baby boy.

Some people say Thây is great, but does not allow a real master-disciple relationship. I don't think it is true. If you allow him to see through you, if you drop your mask and try to inter-be, he becomes your personal teacher. He is part of me now. Although I live very close to Plum Village, I don't feel the need to see him much anymore. Our streams have met and he has colored my waters with beautiful transparent greens and blues.

The Joy of Practice

Chân Tuê Nghiêm

The sun is setting over the horizon. The clouds are turning pink. The birds greet each other good night. The forests are still, silent, and majestic in the evening. The green color carpets the fields around me. I stop by here after a short walking meditation in order to absorb the beauty and serenity of the evening. Breathing in, I am aware I am sitting on a field of grass. Breathing out, I am happy to be alive. Breathing in, I am aware I am sitting on this beautiful earth of France. Breathing out, I smile and feel the joy of being alive.

Over yonder, the stone buildings of Plum Village lie in the silence of the evening. On my way here, I walked in mindfulness, aware of my breath and of my footsteps caressing the earth. Touching this soil of France, I feel very fortunate to be here. What is special about this countryside of France that I have accepted as my home? The answer is Plum Village. Plum Village has become my spiritual home. It is through the teachings of Thây and the support of this community that I have found faith in something beautiful, good and true.

I recall the first time I came to Plum Village two years ago. I was a person without faith. My family did not understand me. I held a big grudge against those who represent my spiritual tradition. I felt overwhelmed and stressed out by my studies. I was an unhappy person, incapable of appreciating what I had, what was around me. During my stay in Plum Village, I have learned to live in the present moment in order to feel my

Thây teaches the children a new hand gesture

existence, my suffering, and my happiness. Every step I take, every smile I make, every breath I breathe, I am making the earth, the trees, the bird songs, the flowers, the blue sky present and real for my own nourishment and joy. I am coming back to the present to enjoy the beauties and nature's wonders that surround me. I am learning just that—smiling, talking, walking, eating, and drinking in mindfulness.

❋
Birthday Present

"In two days, it is going to be Tuê Nghiêm's birthday. What am I going to give her? A cake? Flowers?"

After a long walking meditation, I finally knew what would be the best gift: I would practice loving Tuê Nghiêm as I would practice loving Chou.

Chou is my only younger sister. When she was a baby, I treated her like my living doll. I spoke to her with a lisp, and tried to train her to speak in this way forever. I did not want her to grow up, but she grew up anyway. I did not want there to be any difference between her and me. I always divided candies and cookies with her equally. I forced her to have the same hobbies, tastes, and ways of thinking as me. I tried to mold her personality. Then the day came when I had to live far away from her and I regretted loving her in such a dictatorial way.

This very regret has made me determined to practice Thây's teaching on true love, which is made of understanding. Tuê Nghiêm was my only younger sister in the Dharma (she was born two minutes after me). I do not want to have any regret when the time comes for us to leave each other.

Since then, I have practiced mindfulness to be fully present with my body and mind, to listen deeply to Tuê Nghiêm. I have learned to look deeply in order to understand, to respect her personality and her way of thinking (which are sometimes the opposite of mine). Without expecting anything from her, I often have the tendency to indulge her a little bit. On her birthday, I volunteered to wash all the pots for her after meals (it was her turn to do it as community work). Loving in this way, I feel happier and more free.

Thanks to Thây's teachings, I know more or less how to love and to make up for my mistakes. Chou must be happy to know that she herself has given me the energy to practice in order to transform my selfish love. When I truly love Tuê Nghiêm, I truly love the Chou in me. This is a transformation of my whole habit of living and loving. And this transformation does not make only three of us happy, but many others as well.

—Chân Dinh Nghiêm

My practice is being conscious of my in- and out-breath, my footsteps, my actions, and my thoughts. Yet the happiness and transformations brought about by the mindfulness practice are unbelievable. I have come to accept myself with all my weaknesses as well as my strengths. I no longer run away from my negative feelings and emotions that once overwhelmed and incapacitated me, but come to face them without fear. With mindfulness, I can now embrace them in order to soothe and transform them. I have more confidence and joy in my practice of mindfulness, being aware of my presence and the presence of everything around me.

Walking here this evening, I feel thankful to my parents, family members, and grandparents who have transmitted to me this body, their love and life experience. I feel deep gratitude towards my teachers, friends, and all those who have taught and shown me the way of love and understanding. From them I have learned concrete methods to bring happiness, joy, and peace to me. The trees, the birds, the sunset, the farmers who worked on these fields, and many others have also contributed greatly in making my life possible. Breathing mindfully as I sit here, I feel their energy running through my body. I feel their presence in me. I am smiling to all of them in me.

Now I shall walk back to Plum Village, each step feeling my presence with the earth, each breath smiling to those who have made life, peace, and happiness in me possible. With each mindful step and conscious breath, I shall walk for myself. I shall walk for them all.

Breathing with Mom

Jean-Marc Maquin

At Plum Village I met some friends who helped me in the practice of breathing: trees, flowers, pebbles, clouds, and a smiling child—all members of the Sangha. I also met Thây Nhat Hanh, who taught me how to live in peace, to look deeply into my feelings and transform the unwholesome seeds into good ones, to observe others in order to understand them. "Breathing in, I calm. Breathing out, I smile." This mindfulness practice helps me transform my anger into compassion for the people who contribute to my anger. Of course, I don't succeed every day. But, over time, I have discovered many things that help bring me back to where I really am, the present moment. Sometimes the "bell of mindfulness" is a car horn blowing in the street or a phone ringing or the sound of rain. The examples are numerous, and I am sure you have your own "friends" who can help you as well.

When I came back home after the summer session at Plum Village, my family noticed a difference in me. I was more calm and serene, and it influenced their behavior. What shone in me "inter-was" and supported their states of mind. My mother, who had been the most skeptical and reserved about my spending my summer holidays in a Buddhist center, started coming into my room to discuss how she should respond in various situations.

For a long time now, my mother has taken care of her mother and handicapped brother who live together. It's not always easy and can create tension in the "family's heart." When the anxiety and tension arise, I try to breathe and smile to restore peace in the home. One evening, Mother returned from Grandma's flat with a certain heaviness about her eyes, as though she was in deep suffering. "Your grandmother may have cancer. I will meet with a specialist tomorrow, and he will tell me the details," she said and cried.

I stayed a long time with my mother to comfort her. "Mother," I said, "tomorrow, while you wait your turn in the doctor's office, breathe deeply. Feel the air fill your chest. Be aware of each inhalation and each exhalation, and you will experience the miracle of calm being born in you."

When my mother came back from the doctor's, she thanked me. "I practiced breathing as you suggested, and when my turn came, I felt so peaceful, the doctor could have told me anything and I would have accepted it...even if he told me that my mother had just one year to live."

At this moment, my grandmother is still alive. My mother takes care of her and my uncle. My father has stopped drinking wine during lunch. Harmony in the family is real. I experience it every day!

Jean-Pierre composing a song on his flute

Message

Thich Nhat Hanh

Life has left her footprints on my forehead.
But I have become a child again this morning.
The smile, seen through leaves and flowers,
is back to smooth away the wrinkles,
as the rains wipe away footprints on the beach.
Again a cycle of birth and death begins.

I walk on thorns, but firmly, as among flowers.
I keep my head high.
Rhymes bloom among the sounds of bombs and mortars.
The tears I shed yesterday have become rain.
I feel calm hearing its sound on the thatched roof.
Childhood, my birthland, is calling me,
and the rains melt my despair.

I am still here alive, able to smile quietly.
O sweet fruit brought forth by the tree of suffering!
Carrying the dead body of my brother,
I go across the rice field in the darkness.
Earth will keep you tight within her arms, my dear,
so that tomorrow you will be reborn as flowers,
those flowers smiling quietly in the morning field.
This moment you weep no more, my dear.
We have gone through too deep a night.

This morning,
I kneel down on the grass,
when I notice your presence.
Flowers that carry the marvelous smile of ineffability
speak to me in silence.

The message,
the message of love
and understanding,
has indeed come to us.

Sangha as Teacher

Richard Brady

A high school math teacher for more than twenty years, I began Zen Buddhist practice four years ago. It is the teacher's job to touch the student's deepest desire to practice, so that the work comes from his or her core, realizing great energy. In this state, one is described as having "the mind of enlightenment," or bodhicitta. Thây's beautiful teachings in June 1992 evoked *bodhicitta* in me. I felt the seeds of love, responding to the stimulation of his teachings and the Sangha that had gathered.

A schoolteacher's job is generally not easy. Each student brings a unique history, base, and readiness to receive. In this context, Thây talked about the teacher's role in the Rinzai Zen tradi-

"Mindful movement" exercises

tion. The teacher must understand who the student is and recognize that a particular *kung an* is capable of touching the student's deepest interest and desire to understand. "The math teacher's job," Thây said, "is not to teach the student mathematics, but rather to remove the barriers that prevent the student from learning mathematics." The most serious barriers to learning are the seeds of pain, fear, and suffering. These seeds can erect a wall around the garden of the store consciousness and make it nearly impossible for new, healthy seeds to be planted or old ones to be watered. How can students in this condition be transformed?

Thây also taught us early in the retreat that learning how to benefit from the presence of the Sangha was the most important opportunity the retreat offered. The Dharma talks and the practice were secondary, he said. At Plum Village, Sangha was built in many ways. Affinity groups brought people with common concerns together. Special occasions such as tea ceremonies, formal meals, Plum Village's anniversary celebration, precept recitations, and an ordination ceremony were interspersed throughout the month. At the Dharmacarya Ceremony, the Sangha celebrated the empowerment of nine members as Dharma teachers. Thây also helped build the Sangha in symbolic ways. To emphasize the importance of mutual support, he gave each retreatant an "I walk for you" sticker to put in his or her shoe prior to the first walking meditation. Thây's teaching on interbeing further helped dissolve the distinctions between individual Sangha members. When my practice felt ragged, I could feel the presence of other parts of "myself" practicing beautifully and joyfully, helping me get back on track.

As I reflect on these lessons from Plum Village, I wonder what to do with them. They are not exactly prescriptions for better teaching. They are more like seeds planted deep in my soil. Better teaching will grow naturally as I tend my garden with mindfulness.

Acceptance

Svein Myreng

I was born with a congenital heart disease that has limited my physical activity and more than once has brought me to the brink of death. Mental aspects of this handicap have, on the whole, been hardest to handle. The gap between my wish to be active and the limits set by my heart condition has been difficult at times, but the feeling that my disability made me worthless has been the real problem. I don't know how early in life this feeling started to grow, or why, but I think it has been with me for a long time. It probably was nourished by other people's fear and denial about disease and handicaps, and their aversion to suffering. In my teens, this feeling grew into a wish to hide my heart completely and to restrain my breath carefully, never to sound out-of-breath. I fought hard to pretend that all was well. Carrying my "dark secret," it has taken me many years of meditation to open up.

I believe this is a universal experience. The pressures from society's expectations and hopes—other people's as well as our own—shape us into patterns that do not fit. Our healthy emotional tissue gets scarred by all the cosmetic surgery that is performed on our mind.

After meeting Thây, it became clear to me that practicing acceptance is essential for healing. Acceptance is not fatalistic passivity where we believe that we just have to endure. Acceptance is to acknowledge a situation for what it is and to calm down inside of it. If we then find we can bring about change, very good! If not, then we must acknowledge and accept that. In both cases, a clear, open heart and mind are useful.

Recently I woke up with my heart beating extremely fast and out of rhythm. Though unpleasant physically, I noticed that I didn't feel the strong sense of failure that this illness has triggered in me in the past. I was able to stay calm and reasonably happy, dwelling in the present moment. This felt very satisfying and has given me further trust in mindfulness practice. It also showed that acceptance is very close to patience. Physical or mental pain often brings a burning sense of restlessness. When we can stay aware and not be carried away by it, we can be present and not make things worse by futile attempts to escape that only bring tension and conflict.

Even more useful than accepting difficult situations is accepting our own reactions to them. When our feelings and thoughts are not calm and patient, but rather angry, jealous, or petty, they are often difficult to accept. Our self-image is threatened. It is helpful to remember that thoughts and feelings arise naturally. The question is how we react to them.

The Buddha mentions three ways of reacting that create difficulties. One is escaping from an unpleasant situation into sensual pleasures or fantasy through entertainment, food, sex, or shopping. We lose important opportunities to learn how to cope with difficulties and easily become victims of the many toxins in modern culture. The second way is to cling to experiences. As everything changes, this attitude also removes us from the way things are. The third is to try to block off large parts of ourselves. With concentration, we can become aware of these habits,

The community greets the day together

from the way things are. The third is to try to block off large parts of ourselves. With concentration, we can become aware of these habits, and they will no longer dominate us. Practicing acceptance, we can allow more of our imperfections to be visible. We can learn more about ourselves and walk more lightly through life. This also makes us more tolerant of others. We won't need to project our dark sides onto others, and we become more open-minded.

Accepting and seeing ever more subtle feelings, thoughts, and impulses can be quite a challenge. I sense how I'd like to be perfect and tend not to allow myself much leeway. I can see that both the thirst for situations to go away and the wish to be someone special bring strain and unpleasantness. Slowly, as I accept myself, I let go more and more. We can remember that our internal knots—desire, aversion, ignorance, pride, indecision—are universal. There is no need to blame ourselves for them.

If our intentions are good and honest and we are willing to use difficulties as a way to learn, *The Sutra of Assembled Treasures* has this encouraging comment: "Just as the excrement and garbage disposed by the people living in big cities will yield benefit when placed in vineyards and sugarcane fields, so the residual afflictions of a bodhisattva will yield benefits because they are conducive to all-knowing understanding." Another exercise is to celebrate imperfection instead of seeing it as something undesirable. We acknowledge that life will never be perfect and we can actually enjoy this fact!

On their first visit to Plum Village, many people have difficulties with the simple living conditions, constantly changing schedule, and lack of orderly silence. Both this situation and our reactions to it can be very valuable, as they challenge

BEING AN ISLAND UNTO MYSELF

Be-ing an is-land un-to my-self. As an
is-land un-to my-self. Bud-dha is my
mind-ful-ness. Shin-ing far, shin-ing
near. Dhar-ma is my breath-ing, guard-ing
bo-dy and mind. I am free.
Be-ing an is-land un-to my-self. As an
is-land un-to my-self. San-gha is my
skan-dhas, work-ing in har-mo-ny. Tak-ing
re-fuge in my-self. Com-ing back to myself. I am free, I am free, I am free.

our habits and expectations. I have a hunch that this is one of the reasons why Plum Village allows people to get in touch with deep aspects of themselves so remarkably quickly. (Of course, love, beauty, and a happy atmosphere help.)

The practice of acceptance helps us attain the stillness described in *The Miracle of Mindfulness*: "Once your feelings and thoughts no longer disturb you, at that time mind begins to dwell in mind. Your mind will take hold of mind in a direct and wondrous way, which no longer differentiates between subject and object." We can be alive and cheerful, moving from one moment to the next, shedding our sorrows as we go.

Mindful Medical Work

Jørgen Hannibal

I have recently returned to working as a general medical practitioner. In doing so, I have benefited from the teachings of Thây in the following ways:

I do some form of walking meditation while going from one room to the other. My office has two doors leading to the room where I meet the patient. On my side of the door, I have taped a small drawing of a smiling face that reminds me to take three mindful breaths before going through the door, and maybe even to smile. This helps me be more aware of the attitude I have towards the patient, and I can be more present when I meet the patient. Trying to be aware of the Buddha nature of each patient—whether she be a beautiful girl with a sore throat, or a chronic, foul-smelling alcoholic coming for the thousandth time to detoxify—is a great help.

My work has also shown me that the doors of my heart are not as open as I might think. I am often more concerned with my own comfort and needs than with the needs of the patients and coworkers. In realizing this, I try to breathe and smile so as not to create a battlefield within myself.

Recently, working as a doctor in Sweden, I was on call for twenty-four hours in the emergency room. At some point, I was eating my lunch, and I became aware of the physical and mental tension present in me. I directed my attention to my in-breath and out-breath, and I realized there was no difference in the process of eating while on-call in the emergency room or while sitting at a calm lakeside. Eating became much more pleasant as I really ate my bread and banana and stopped eating my tension. I then became aware of my mind ruminating with my experience and composing a piece for this book, and I smiled.

Somewhere in Buddhist literature I have read about the importance of cultivating the capacity to be silent and to refrain from interfering. On the other hand, there are situations that call for action with right mindfulness, right understanding, and skillful means. Recently I found myself in a situation calling for professional action —but I did not act. Afterwards I felt ashamed of myself for not having acted. I felt the creation of "internal formations" and karma. In processing what took place, the teachings of Thây and the Buddha helped me. The situation is gone, and only as part of the past is it present. Only as such can I change it by the way I process what happened. The part of me responsible for not having acted adequately is still the part of me deserving loving kindness, compassion, and forgiveness. I am not just the part that did not act; I am more than that. I experience how the unwholesome action represents energy that can be transformed and, as compost, fertilize the growth of beautiful flowers.

Smiling

Chân Phâp Dâng

In Plum Village, our mindfulness practice is the practice of joy and happiness. Everything we do here is to cultivate joy and happiness, and the foundation of our joy and happiness is the capacity of smiling. We practice smiling in every look, in every step, and in every breath.

Practicing mindfulness without a smile makes us feel heavy, tired and bored, and very soon we abandon our practice. Sometimes people feel overwhelmed because of their unjoyful practice. It is not always easy to smile. But if we continuously practice smiling, it becomes a habit. The

Little Bamboo entertains the community with her beautiful violin-playing

more we smile, the happier we are. Every morning when I wake up, I go back to my breathing and recite this gatha:

> *Waking up this morning, I smile.*
> *Twenty-four brand new hours are before me.*
> *I vow to live fully in each moment.*
> *I vow to look at all beings with the eyes*
> *of compassion.*

Just reciting this gatha while breathing consciously, a smile comes easily to my lips. Sometimes I forget to smile but when I open the window, the birds singing remind me.

During sitting meditation, I establish myself firmly in my conscious breathing and I smile. Joy and happiness are always there but we have to recognize them, and a smile makes it easy. Living as a young monk with a beautiful Sangha and feeling calm in the practice of sitting is very pleasant. Joy and happiness spring up naturally through my smiling. My smile brings joy and happiness into the atmosphere of my Sangha and I can feel it.

In the morning, we greet each other with an early smile, and we also welcome our guests with a big smile. Before leaving us, an American friend said, "Thank you for your support in the practice, especially your smile. It has made a great change in me."

We usually eat our meals in silence. From time to time we look up at our Sangha and smile. I usually smile in the formal meal because my younger sister Chân Tuê Nghiêm sits right in front of me. I like to eat in silence because I can touch the food deeply. Just eating rice, feelings of joy and happiness arise in me. I see my brothers and sisters in Vietnam through the rice. Feeling like this makes the food more precious and tasty.

In guided meditation, we practice smiling to our bodies, our feelings, our pain, and our anger because a smile has the power to heal and to calm our feelings, our pain, and our anger, and to nourish our joy and happiness. A smile is a flower and it can blossom on the lips of everyone.

❋
Happiness

Someone asked me, "Why do you want to become a monk?" I replied, "I don't want to become a monk, I want to be a monk." The day I was ordained, I said to my mother, "I have the feeling our whole family that is being ordained."

Since then, I feel at home, no longer a wanderer. When a person cannot stop wishing to become something or someone else, the quality of his happiness is very poor. I used to think that to have happiness I needed a good job, a good car, and so on. But I don't have any of those things, and I experience a lot of happiness. The conditions to be happy—my mother's love, my family's happiness, real friendship—were always there, but I did not know how to cherish them. The things we have been looking for are often within our reach. We only need to see them.

—Chân Pháp Dung

Sister Chân Không on the balcony of Golden Years Hut

The World Today

Bruce Ho

Sun shines brighter than the sky.
It bursts through the clouds.
Capture it in your hand.
Turn the world round and round.
It's time to look around you.
See the land change every season.
Look around once more.
There is more than this continent.
Explore the world.
Let the sun shine brightly,
Let it see the stars.
Time after time, day after day,
conserve energy.
Let sunlight warm up your senses.
Turn around in a circle.
See the sights again.
Find yourself in the present moment.
Don't think about the future.
Let your senses shine.
Smell the flowers, eat the fruit, touch the sky.
See the world around you,
Let them move your heart.
Look and tell the tale.
Tell it in it's full length.
Details are important.
The story will tell itself.
Unless we keep polluting,
it's time for the greatest change of all eternity!
Take the daybreak course
in the midst of the clouds.
Time is not important.
Just let your ideas spin.
Justice and eternity
roll down the streets,
waiting to be caught.
Here is today,
Our only hope for tomorrow!

Inviting the Dragon to Tea

Eveline Beumkes

Since I first invited Sister Jina to come to Holland after I moved from Plum Village to Amsterdam, my life has been filled with organizing Sangha activities. I have finally found something that I can do with all my heart, without the least bit of resistance. I wouldn't want to do anything else. But I have not yet managed to do whatever presents itself in a lighthearted way. There are always so many things to do, and they all seem equally urgent. The pile on my desk never gets down to the point where I feel it is manageable. It often burdens me. I feel no space. I often feel I am not in touch enough with the present and the joy that it contains. I know how incongruent this is with the work I am doing.

So this is what I have to look deeply into—the way I work. It has to do with a lot of other things—how I deal with or avoid my feelings, the need to manifest myself in some way, the wish to please others, and so on. I have always felt an intense dread of being responsible and have wished to hide from that role. I run away in fear and feel chased by responsibilities. But lately another attitude has opened up in me, a willingness to turn around and face what is chasing me, saying to responsibility, "Here I am."

Recently I began therapy with a woman a little older than myself who is a big sister and friend to me as well. In her presence, I am not ashamed or afraid of the difficult, hidden feelings that arise in me. Recently, I found myself asking, "What am I doing here?" I thought I was done with this ques-

tion a long time ago, that its bones had turned to dust already, that the despair it brought up belonged to the past. Since meeting Thây, his teachings have given me more and more ground to stand on, dissolving the problem about the meaning of life. I thought this question had become irrelevant.

Handmade sign welcomes visitors to the Upper Hamlet

But the question was still alive in the dark *alaya*-earth and it became unearthed during one session with my therapist. She started the session as usual by playing some soft music to bring me in closer touch with my feelings. This time, the music brought me back to the time I nearly always felt depressed, when I wondered intensely and relentlessly what my purpose was in life. The emptiness I felt was breathtaking.

Preparing a vegetarian meal in mindfulness

I realized that the question, "What am I doing here?" presents an overwhelming emptiness that has been a seven-headed dragon swallowing all my joy. I had assumed that this dragon had starved to death because I had not given him anything to eat for a long time. But I discovered that he has secret food reserves that I didn't know about. I decided to invite him to tea.

My therapist joined me at this tea, asking me, "How do you answer the question, 'What am I doing here?' in this moment?" I could not answer. With all the Sangha-building activities that bring me joy and give me the feeling I am doing meaningful work, I could not answer the question.

Then one answer surfaced: "I am waiting for 'X' to appear." "X" is the person I think of as "my beloved" but whom I haven't seen for years. There is still the dream of having someone to whom I can hand over the heavy burden of be-i ng responsible for my life. It is a dream that shines light on my desire to hide away from responsibility.

"'What am I doing here?' seems to be a very important question in your life," my therapist said. "It belongs to you just as much as your heart or your liver does. The question is very much Eveline, irrespective of the answer."

I felt soothed by these words. This question has lived in me since I was a child. I have always treated it as an unwanted guest because it scared me. I was looking for life, and death grinned at me when I allowed this question to come up. Suddenly, I saw this question as a mere question. After years of hearing it in dreadful awe and pushing it away, I could receive the question as it is—a question, a peer, and not an oppressive, fear-inducing dragon. I even regret that I have treated it so badly. And, I began to feel proud of it, respecting it as an important part of me.

During the week since that session, I bring it to mind often with a smile. There is no chasing after any answer, just an invitation to the question to sit there, with space around it, and to give attention to it. I just smile at the question and experience the moment as it is.

Building Sangha

Richard Baker

The Buddhist Sangha is one of the oldest continuing institutions in the world. It represents the potential or capacity of a society to live together—if a few people can find a way to live together, then many people can find a way to live together. It is this effort and example, rather than the scale of its success, that offer a society a model and an opportunity to deepen its expression. A community can give us the space and support needed to express ourselves individually and with others in the simplest, most adequate way.

The physical care and expression of our situation and life are very important in Zen practice. The bonding aspect of a Buddhist community is that we meditate together and share a daily practice, which produces a common life. Meditation is both a mode for personal change and the provider of a deep sense of openness and space that reduce many of the problems that naturally occur in community.

The actual physical space is an important part of what makes people able to live together and develop the bonds of community. The bells, drums, and sounding boards of a Buddhist community articulate and relate space and events. The visual space should be varied, related, and if possible visually interlocking. The space of physical passage should be designed according to what will be done there—people walking slowly and quietly, for example. Stone walkways can bring you the long way around a building so that you change your pace and enter the building with familiarity. Passage within and between buildings can be designed according to how often people will meet each other and the significance of the activities and buildings joined by the passage.

Work is an essential part of the practice in a Zen community. It is the way we spend time together and take care of the needs of our environmental and social existence. The work we do together is too valuable to sacrifice to machines or the saving of time.

Our society, if it is to survive, needs every kind of community. In the West, the identity and good

Thầy Giác Thanh on the porch of Floating Clouds Hut

of the individual has been given such singular priority that every association is seen as serving the individual. Few people understand or act through the responsibility of association and mutuality. Community represents that compassionate good will and realistic regard for others and ourselves that establishes and maintains a humane social order. It is the natural expression and necessary basis of real freedom.

The Old Mendicant

Thich Nhat Hanh

Being rock, being gas, being mist, being Mind,
being the mesons travelling among the galaxies at the speed of light,
you have come here, my beloved.
And your blue eyes shine, so beautiful, so deep.
You have taken the path traced for you
from the non-beginning and the never-ending.
You say that on your way here
you have gone through many millions of births and deaths.
Innumerable times you have been transformed
into firestorms in outer space.
You have used your own body
to measure the age of the mountains and rivers.
You have manifested yourself
as trees, grass, butterflies, single-celled beings, and as chrysanthemums.
But the eyes with which you look at me this morning
tell me that you have never died.
Your smile invites me into the game whose beginning no one knows,
the game of hide-and-seek.

O green caterpillar, you are solemnly using your body
to measure the length of the rose branch that grew last Summer.
Everyone says that you, my beloved, were just born this Spring.
Tell me, how long have you been around?
Why wait until this moment to reveal yourself to me,
carrying with you that smile which is so silent and so deep?
O caterpillar, suns, moons, and stars flow out each time I exhale.
Who knows that the infinitely large must be found in your tiny body?
Upon each point on your body,
thousands of Buddha fields have been established.
With each stretch of your body, you measure time
from the non-beginning to the never-ending.
The great mendicant of old is still there on Vulture Peak,
contemplating the ever-splendid sunset.

Gautama, how strange! Who said that the Udumbara flower blooms
only once every 3,000 years?
The sound of the rising tide—you cannot help hearing it
if you have an attentive ear.

A Joyful Path

Chân Không

When Ursula was fifteen, she left home. A friend of her family had sexually abused her, and no one seemed to understand or sympathize. She moved to another country, found a job, and began to go to school; but for years she cried every night. She felt angry and afraid every time she thought of her parents.

Ursula came to Plum Village and practiced sitting meditation, walking meditation, and touching-the-earth prostrations. She began to read many books by Thây Nhat Hanh, and continued to practice looking deeply. After just four months, her heart was soothed, and she decided to visit her parents to attempt to make peace.

Her parents welcomed her, and she opened her heart to them. But they were not able to listen. Feeling lost, she decided to leave forever, but she fell ill and could not leave. She wrote to me at Plum Village describing her frustration, and I phoned right away. During our conversation, she could feel the energy of the Plum Village Sangha supporting her, and she determined: "I have to make peace now or never."

Still sick in bed, she asked her mother for a cup of tea. As her mother handed it to her, Ursula held onto her hand and asked her mother to tell her about the suffering she had endured. Her mother began crying uncontrollably and began to share stories of the hidden pain she and her husband had undergone for many years. The more Ursula listened, the more she began to feel the water of compassion spring forth within her. She had been so immersed in her own pain that she had not even noticed her parents' difficulties. During the next few days, Ursula's parents made a dear friend in their daughter, and finally they were able to listen to her story. In tears they hugged one another and found real mutual trust. Ursula is now happy and at ease with her tradition, her family, and her new job. On my desk is a large photo of Ursula and her parents smiling beautifully.

I met Robert at a retreat in England. He was as sad as a wounded bird, but when he looked at Thây, his blue eyes radiated sunshine. We invited him to practice at Plum Village, and he agreed. For two years, he followed the methods of looking deeply offered by Thây, and his transformation was thorough. He told me that at the age of five, he had felt jealous when his mother gave birth to another child, and he ran away from home on the inside. He became a difficult child, especially for his father, who began to beat him and speak harshly to him. When Robert grew up, he received several advanced degrees and then studied Buddhism in India for seven years, but he still did not know how to be happy.

At Plum Village he learned to understand and accept his father. The guided meditation on looking at one's father as a five-year-old child helped him very much. He learned to recognize and say hello to his jealousy, his fear, and his sadness each time they arose in him, and as a result, he now smiles very often. He is a dear friend and inspiration to many people.

There are so many stories like these. I have seen people who, after just three weeks of listening to Dharma talks and living in the community, have become fresh as flowers. Thây Nhat Hanh says, "There is no way to happiness. Happiness is the way." I hope you will join us on this joyful path of practice.

True Goodness

Lyn Fine

Amidst the trees along the walking path
    of the Upper Hamlet
I sit on a rock.
You too are here,
You are the trees.
You are the rock.
You are the gentle cool breeze across my cheek.

In this moment
I am aware
I touch your love.

I am the rock.
I am the trees.
I am the gentle cool breeze across your cheek.

I am grateful we meet.
    Here, now—in myriad forms.
    This morning at tea.
    Twelve years ago, June 1982.
    The Reverence for Life Conference in New York City
    To end the production and distribution of nuclear weapons.

Breathing and smiling
    I cultivate joy.
    I am solid as a mountain,
    I touch equanimity again,
    Step out of fear and anxiety.

Writing this sentence, I hear the sound of a car.
    The car drives past where I am sitting.
    You are there, you are here.
    We smile and meet, touching eyes.
    The car drives on.

The mind has its commentary: "There are no accidents."

Thank you, dear friend.

More Good News

Marci Thurston-Shaine

The good news exists,
often twisted and obscure.
We try to print and live it right.
Each of us is a special edition, every moment
new ink wet behind our ears.
The good news is being alive, changing,
knowing the linden tree stands there, changing,
yet strong through many harsh winters.
The good news is your eyes
that touch the blue sky, the cloud
The good news is the child before me,
my arms available.
Hugging is possible.
So often news is tangled and wrong.
Please look at the special edition
that I offer every moment,
and tell me if I am wrong or hurtful.
The dandelion is there
in a crack in the sidewalk,
smiling her wondrous smile,
singing her song of eternity.
Lo! You have ears capable of hearing
and a voice capable of song.
Bow your head, and listen to her.
Sing to her.
You and I are flowers of a tenacious family.
Breathe slowly and deeply,
free of previous occupation.
The latest good news
is that you can do it,
and that I can take time to do it too, with you.

PLUM VILLAGE is a meditation community in southwestern France, where Thich Nhat Hanh leads a year-round program of meditation practice for residents and for visitors who come for at least one week. The Summer Opening is from July 15 to August 15. Please write in advance to:

Registrar
Plum Village
Meyrac
47120 Loubès-Bernac
France

PARALLAX PRESS was founded in 1985 to publish books on socially engaged Buddhism. We now have 75 books in print, including *The Plum Village Chanting Book*; *Learning True Love*, by Chân Không, and *Being Peace*, *Touching Peace*, and 20 other books by Thich Nhat Hanh. For a copy of our free catalog, please write to:

Parallax Press
P.O. Box 7355
Berkeley, CA 94707
USA